THANKS FOR SHARING

T0000010

THANKS FOR SHARING

How I Gave Up Buying and
Embraced Swapping, Borrowing and Renting

Eleanor Tucker

Aurum

First published in 2023 by Aurum, an imprint of
The Quarto Group.
One Triptych Place,
London, SE1 9SH.
United Kingdom

T (0)20 7700 6700
www.Quarto.com/Aurum
Text copyright © 2023 Eleanor Tucker
Design copyright © 2023 Quarto Publishing plc

A catalogue record for this book is available from the British Library.

ISBN 978-0-7112-8218-6
E-book ISBN 978-0-7112-8220-9
Audiobook ISBN 978-0-7112-8598-9

10 9 8 7 6 5 4 3 2 1

Typeset in Melior LT Std by SX Composing DTP Ltd

Printed by CPI Group (UK) Ltd, Croydon, CR0 4YY

For Jake and Phoebe

Contents

Stop right there

This is not a business book. If you're after something technical on marketplaces, platforms or online communities I admire you, but I don't think you should read this. Stop now, put the book down and head to the other end of the shop. Or, if you're online, go back a page and return to your search. Thank you. You see the thing is, there are plenty of books out there about digital transformation and suchlike, and a lot of them are brilliant. But I haven't written one of those. Because although I work in this world, and had the urge to write about the sharing economy, I knew from the start that it wasn't going to be *that* kind of book. Why? Quite honestly, I'm not *that* kind of person.

Instead, I wanted to write something that answers not my colleagues' questions, but those of my friends and family. And what they often ask me is 'HOW?' and 'WHY?' and 'IS THAT REALLY A THING?' and 'YOU DID WHAT??'. (Not all of these questions relate to the sharing economy.) Quite often, they're not sure what it is, let alone how it works in real life. And I guessed that if my friends and family aren't sure about it, then a lot of other people aren't either.

So I wrote this book as a way of saying *this* is what it's all about. This is the version of the sharing economy that isn't in the business section of the bookshop: it's on your phone, it's on your laptop or your tablet – if you want it to be. These are some of the apps and platforms you can try, and here's why – and how – you might want to. Some of them work (for me), some of them don't work as well (again, for me). Some of them are weird, some of them are brilliant and I'll never stop using them, and some of them are probably not worth the effort for everyone. Some of them just need a few more years to get going, so bear with them. And here's the really exciting part: I'm going to try some of them for you, like a sharing economy guinea pig. I'm also going to tell you a bit about why I think most of them are a good idea, and when and where a lot of the ideas for them came from in the first place (spoiler alert: it was usually a *very* long time ago).

––––

Let's not get ahead of ourselves. First of all, what even *is* the sharing economy? Put simply, it's using technology – in the form of an app or an online platform – to connect with other people (rather than businesses) to borrow, rent or swap instead of buying. In other words, it's anything which could be described as 'the Airbnb of . . .' (although I'm not a fan of that phrase, you'll find out why a bit later), like listing your clothes on a website for others to borrow, or renting a car from your neighbour via an app. It's also easily confused with similar terms, like the circular economy, which the sharing economy *can* be part of but is more generally about keeping materials in use for as long as possible by reuse and recycling.

A bit of recent history: the phrase 'sharing economy' was used for the first time by a Harvard professor in 2008, and in 2011 it was described by *Time* magazine as one of the 'Ten Ideas That Will Change the World'. Quite a lot to live up to. Since then, the concept has been lauded as much as it has been criticised, misunderstood as much it has been analysed, declared 'dead on arrival' (often next to pictures of piles of abandoned bikes or scooters) and confused with loads of other 'trends'. Many early sharing platforms and apps did indeed fall by the wayside, with no similar companies to learn from and potential customers that didn't necessarily even get the idea in the first place. Some people just didn't like the idea of sharing things with others, maybe they thought – or think – that it's unhygienic, or not 'exclusive' enough. Which doesn't really make sense – hotel beds, even in the most expensive suites, were slept in by someone else the night before you checked in, so are 'shared' in that sense, just like cinema or restaurant seats.

There were other challenges: regulations, building trust, the technology that made the whole thing easy, finding insurance . . . even just knowing what the right 'things' were to share. But now, a decade and a half later, after failures and successes, the resulting apps and platforms are widely available for us to use, in most countries in the world. Some of them have even become 'unicorns' (a startup company with a value of over $1 billion). But that's getting into business talk, and I said I wouldn't do that.

So what are the benefits of these 'peer-to-peer' or 'person-to-person' – rather than 'business-to-consumer'

– transactions? There are more than you might think. Firstly, they allow us to get more use from things (or 'assets') that we don't use very much, or don't use at all. The fact is, the world has too many things in it, and, at the risk of overusing the word 'things', when people transact with one another rather than a business, and share use of the same 'thing', it slows down the production of more of these things. That's why another name for the sharing economy is 'collaborative consumption', which I like as a term, but mainly because of the alliteration.

It's not only 'things' you can share. Sharing skills or services on online platforms and apps allows people to use themselves, or the things they can do, as an 'asset'. For example, you could share skills to make money, or in some cases, trade or swap them for credits to buy other skills and services. I get into this later in the book, and by way of a teaser, Henry the Hoover is involved, and there is a bold mention of nipple tassels. This is one of only a couple of risqué things in the whole book, making it appropriate for any age, much like the sharing economy itself.

I digress. In the sharing economy, the choice – and freedom – belongs to the platform or app users. Which leads us to another benefit: empowerment. Teach French five hours a week, because that's what works for you. Clear out your shed and make money by lending out your tools. Hire out your camper van instead of leaving it to sit on your driveway. No camper van? Rent out your driveway: it's up to you. But what I think is the true power of the sharing economy is even more exciting than all of this – and is the part I love the most. Sharing platforms and apps match users and providers, or 'sharers' and 'sharees', both locally and globally, offline and online, so that communities have the chance to thrive again. We become networked: connected to our peers, looking up, down, sideways and around us for exactly what we want or need – not just in a single direction, for a one-size-fits-all delivery from a big business.

————

So that's the sharing economy . . . but what about just *sharing*? Because the thing is, sharing (the sort without the technology part) is something we have always done, as you will hopefully find out in this book. And I mean *always*: some of the examples I've managed to get my hands on go back to the beginning of human history. It has proved itself in the past to be not only *desirable* to collaborate when it comes to consumption, but *essential*. And even (get this) actually part of our evolution. As powerful as that is as a concept, somewhere along the way we stopped sharing as much, and this coincided with us having less of a sense of community, and less of a need, as more things were available to us, thanks to mass production.

There are social commentators who believe that the 'privatisation' of our social lives into smaller units, and the easy availability of technology to choose when and how we use them, has undermined 'social capital' – the collective identity and activity which used to be reflected in things like churches, sports clubs and pubs. So, compared to our parents and grandparents, you could argue that we have very few common experiences. After all, the latter fought in wars and had their diets decided by rations; the former had a very limited choice of media, lifestyle and education compared to young people today. Certain common activities which used to be thought of as essential – like voting – are now considered almost voluntary. Even the common activities we have, like national days and religious festivals, are often presented in a consumerist way. Some people bemoan this, while others celebrate the choice and diversity it brings. So is the sharing economy in fact 'Sharing 2.0'? A new sort of sharing, which is by choice rather than by obligation: 'bite-size', transactional sharing rather than lifelong, inherited identity – and global too, thanks to technology?

However we define it, to me it feels like the stars are aligned for the sharing economy to become mainstream. But as I said before, many people aren't sure how to be part of it, or what it even is. Firstly, it's not about composting your own poo or going to live in a badger's sett: I'm no hippie, although I used to have my nose pierced and experimented heavily with the 'Boho look' in the Noughties. No, this is 'lite' green, about small changes to our day-to-day lives. About doing things like we used to, just taking the good bits with the help of technology. About living more sustainably, making – or saving – some money, and creating powerful connections, online and off.

In part one of this book, 'It's the little things', I'm going to be sharing everyday things: food, clothes, pets, household items and furniture. I start with food, and you get a whole chapter on that. Then you'll be with me as I bring in a new type of sharing at the start of each chapter, and try to embrace it, as per the title of this book. So by the end of part one, I'll have tried all five, and be ready to move on to the bigger things. Then in part two, 'The big idea', I look at how – and why – we can share the larger things in our lives like transport, space, travel, skills and even experiences.

It's not a precise science, but then neither is the sharing economy. As I begin the book, I start doing some sharing things, then bring in new things to try. Some I do once or twice, while other things I keep doing and I'm still doing, because I like them. Some types of sharing are more 'occasional use', and some are a day-to-day activity. So it's more of an 'ebb and flow' than a month-by-month affair, although the book does take place over roughly a year. I'm also not being a total purist: a few areas of the sharing economy have traditional renting mixed in, and that's pretty good too. It'll make more sense when you start reading, but it's explained on the cover when it says 'swapping, borrowing and renting'.

And finally, remember as you read that not all of these platforms and apps will be available where you live (yet), and sometimes you'll actually have access to more of them than I do. To help you try out any of them that appeal to you, I've put some useful information on each type of sharing at the end of each of the two sections of the book. One last thing, I can't try everything – this book would have to be six volumes long if I did, and nobody wants that. Right, are you ready? OK, I'm off to start sharing. You'll thank me, I promise.

Part One

It's the little things

'25 bananas, in a total state'

Like most fridges, ours has two drawers at the bottom, which I believe are known as 'salad drawers'. The drawers in my fridge, however, rarely contain salad, and are generally used as a hiding place for food which is, as my grandmother would have said, 'on the turn'. There are three reasons I do this. Firstly, my husband has no mercy for anything even approaching its Use By date: I can only imagine this is from some childhood trauma involving out-of-date Spam. So I have created a safe haven in the fridge 'basement' for anything that is, to put it politely, 'geriatric' in food terms. Or maybe I should say 'advanced in age'. Or 'venerable'.

The second reason is that as much as I try, I am a terrible housekeeper. I like the fun parts, like baking a Nigella recipe on a rainy Sunday afternoon. Or misting my temperamental houseplants. Or decluttering the Lego box and arranging everything in it by colour. But these fun, spontaneous parts of running a family home don't take into account things like Use By dates. Which is why I also use the bottom of the fridge to hide things I am embarrassed about purchasing on a whim, and then not using. A decaying bag of watercress that I bought for a recipe, then forgot where the recipe was (or what the recipe was). A crab I just couldn't resist when I walked past a fishmonger's but, when it came to cooking it, I got side-tracked by oh, I don't know, *Schitt's Creek*? Or a huge cylindrical goat's cheese, reeking like a middle-aged man's gym bag, which, on closer examination, I couldn't really think *how* to use, at that size and level of pungency.

The third reason is that, and this may come as a surprise having read reasons one and two, I hate wasting food. I often imprison in these drawers a solitary potato wrapped in clingfilm (which would be useful for what exactly?), some fried onions in a small Tupperware pot, or a blackened avocado half which, despite its colour, I am determined to use for tomorrow's lunch. But this will not happen, and said items will see out their remaining edible days in the bottom drawers of the fridge, before they are predictably thrown in the bin three weeks later by my husband as he searches, to a soundtrack of muttering, for the mayonnaise (which is hiding in plain sight on the middle shelf). And off they go to landfill, along with the 900 million tonnes of food thrown away every year globally. That's 17 per cent of the food available to consumers – and 60 per cent of it is from households, just like ours.[1]

And as much I like to think of myself as a frugal wartime housewife, making a roast chicken last the entire week, pickling garden vegetables and doing inventive things with tripe (all the while wearing a morale-boosting slick of red

---

1 www.unep.org

lippie and a figure-enhancing apron) – the reality is that while I have good intentions and feel genuinely appalled to hear that we waste so much food, when it comes to it, it seems like hard work to do things differently. A roast chicken never has a lot of meat left on it the next day, I don't have any vegetables in my garden to pickle (just a postage stamp-size lawn that's mainly buttercups), and I've just googled tripe and it's a 'hard pass'.

———

So when – and why – did food waste first become a problem? Surprisingly, not due to environmental concerns, but simply because everyone was scared of running out. At the beginning of the last century, the Women's Institute was set up in the UK during the First World War with combating food waste as one of its original goals, while in the US at the same time, regulations came in to prevent wastage. During the Second World War', along with rationing, laws were introduced that made wasting food punishable by imprisonment, with advertising campaigns encouraging 'thrifty' cooking and feeding animals with leftovers.

After the war, 'thriftiness' became a thing of the past and as lifestyles changed, less food was cooked from scratch and more people ate out in restaurants and bought convenience food with a shorter shelf life. Wastage started to become the norm and food was thrown away with the rest of our rubbish, ending up in landfill sites. Which isn't just a huge waste of money and resources, it also has a negative impact on the environment too. Food in landfills all over the world breaks down and releases methane, a greenhouse gas twenty-five times more potent than carbon dioxide.

In fact, if it were a country, this wasted food would be the third highest emitter of greenhouse gases in the world.

The good news is that people are starting to wake up to food waste, with campaigns by charities and supermarkets, TV shows encouraging people to use leftovers, more access to food waste recycling bins and better labelling to stop items being thrown out unnecessarily. But a lot more has to be done when waste levels are so high in the first place. The campaigns tell us not to 'overbuy' and keep track of what we've bought and used. 'Shelfies' are encouraged: taking a photo of fridges and cupboards to remind us of what's there. We're also advised to plan ahead, check Use By dates and only buy what we can eat before it expires, as well as think about how we'll use leftovers. Weekends are apparently to be used to batch-cook and freeze meals.

None of which really sounds like something I would do, realistically, any more than I would pickle something or eat tripe. Weekends pass in a blur of child-ferrying, family-visiting, socialising, attempts at cleaning and hopefully, the odd blast of fresh air. Not batch-cooking or shelfie-taking. But I'm painfully aware that people like me are ignoring the issue, as we throw another bag of out-of-date 'washed and ready to eat' salad in the bin and turn our heads away as it begins its journey towards, not our bellies, but a vile, methane-producing heap of thoughtlessness and apathy. Which is, coincidentally, what I often call my thirteen-year-old son Jake's bedroom.

So it's time to try food sharing. Yes, I'm going to share my food, and 'borrow' other people's. Although I get that 'borrow' isn't the right word here, as I won't be giving it back – I'll be eating it. Food sharing, like most other types of sharing, isn't new, but has been revived by technology, and is making a real difference to the food waste problem. It works like this: individuals with leftover food, or 'over-bought' items going to waste, can list them via an app and make them available to people nearby. The beauty of this is that even if you didn't batch-bake all day on Sunday, or meticulously meal plan, you can still prevent food from ending up in the methane/apathy pit. And, like many sharing economy activities, it could also help you save some money, and allow you to explore possibilities that you haven't before. Food sharing apps connect you to other people nearby with food to share, and also to restaurants, food shops and cafés with leftover stock – creating, just like many other sharing apps, an online community. The idea is simply this: to direct food to where it should be – human digestive systems – and keep it out of landfill. If this means that you can get your hands on some free grub: bonus. And for those on lower incomes, the apps can have a positive impact on monthly food spend.

I'm not saying that we shouldn't use other methods of avoiding food waste, if we can. It's just that for now, for me, trying out food sharing will be the order of the day. Frankly, the odds feel slightly stacked against me. Like Joey Tribbiani, my husband 'doesn't share food', and is also genuinely confused about the concept. My son Jake seems convinced we will be eating out-of-date Subway sandwiches from now on and my eleven-year-old daughter Phoebe is making plans to move in with her best friend for the duration. This should be interesting.

———

I get started by downloading a food sharing app. The premise of this one is simple: it connects those who have food they don't want or need, with neighbours who would like it. Users take a picture of their items and list them on the app – locals then receive customised alerts and can request anything that takes their fancy. I register, which is as easy as any other app and free to use, and I'm delighted to read that there are 11,000 users near me. That seems a lot, and I wonder how near is near in this context, so I use the map function rather than the list of food being shared to see what's really near me, here in Edinburgh's Southside. Sure enough, there are users not just on my street but a few doors away, which fills me with excitement.

I set up my profile, using a smiley photo. I'm then asked to describe myself. I look at other people's profiles which are fairly short and sweet and go for 'New to food sharing – a busy mum keen to waste less!' which, thanks to the exclamation mark, seems slightly needy and hysterical, but what else could I say? 'Wasteful beyond belief. Leaves food to rot in her salad drawer'? There is also the option to add likes and dislikes. Under 'likes', the suggestion is 'Rockets or butterflies?', and under 'dislikes' it suggests 'Hailstorms or ants?'. I wonder if they are asking if I like them to eat and ponder over what a battered butterfly would taste like. Chicken, perhaps. I skip the likes and dislikes and head back to the listings, which are divided into two categories, 'food' and 'non-food', the latter due to the fact that this app has also become popular with people sharing unwanted household items. But I'm not here for a 'Broken felt clothes hanger, suitable for a craft project', or indeed Season one of *Scrubs* on DVD. No, I'm here for the grub.

Someone called Ella has listed some gravy granules ('half left') – and she's only 0.4 miles away! After a rush of excitement I remember the children don't like gravy since that time I added port (ironically to avoid wasting it). Scrolling down, Anna has some celery up for grabs about three streets away, and there is also an out-of-date Mother's Pride loaf, some lemon juice and 'An Assorted Bag of Nando's Sauce Sachets'. I wonder if, presented with this selection on a TV cooking challenge show, I could make a meal out of it all that my family might eat. Peri Peri Celery on Toast, anyone?

Feeling a little disheartened – and then side-tracked for an hour or two clearing out the cupboards and fridge to see if I have anything worth listing – I return to my phone to find it lighting up like the proverbial Christmas tree. 'Take a look . . . 4 new food listings near you' (accompanied by the two staring eyes emoji), 'Wowzers – someone is having a clear out' and 'Yum – 20 food listings near you'. I dive onto the app to see a completely different selection of food available than an hour before: Jeff is giving away an aubergine, Paola has listed a Bakewell Tart, and Sandra has '25 bananas, in a total state' that she's keen to part with. Now these I *could* do something with: Aubergines Parmesan, Bakewell Tart for pudding . . . and those unfortunate bananas sound like they'd be perfect for that cake made famous by lockdown: banana bread.

My excitement is short-lived: by the time I've made a cup of tea and sat down with a notebook to do some meal planning, these treasures have already gone. I'm starting to get it: food sharing is not for the slow of scrolling. You snooze, you lose out on the gravy granules ('half left'). Of course: because food is perishable, the listings change by the hour, even the minute – not by the week like Airbnb, which is embarrassingly the only sharing economy platform I've ever used. Every day is a school day in the sharing economy, so I go into my notifications and make sure they are turned up to maximum effect: banners, sounds, badges – the lot. I'm not missing out on Jeff's aubergine again.

———

Now to get listing. After my clear-out I've managed to find a few things that would otherwise imminently be heading for landfill. First up is a bunch of white radishes that came in our organic vegetable box delivery. Nobody in our house likes radishes, and least of all white ones, which appear to be radishes masquerading as turnips: a terrifying vegetable subterfuge. I put them on the table for their photoshoot.

Joining them is a packet of 'Seed Mix'; a pouch of micro-waveable refried beans; vacuum-packed daal; and some wholewheat noodles, all probably purchased on a whim after reading an article about how good legumes/pulses/wholegrains are for you. Then, to make sure I have a steady stream of items to list, and that nothing edible goes into landfill (I could try to pretend here we have a food recycling container, but I think we all know that's not true), I place a box by the bin. I make a sign for it using the back of an algebra worksheet and a purple glitter pen. It reads 'PUT EDIBLE THINGS IN HERE'. Back to the app, I ask potential sharers to message me with a time that suits and then take flattering photos of the items, including close-ups of the Use By dates, and, for the radishes, several angles, one with the leaves flicked over the radishes themselves in a coquettish manner. Who will be able to resist any of this?

Hundreds of people, it seems. The listings go live, and then, like the Eurovision scoreboard, I see my items go up on the app, and next to them, how many people are viewing them. As an hour ticks by, the viewing scores go up and up, the flirtatious radishes attracting the most, a solid 362 no less (and even one like!). The vacuum-packed daal is the least popular, with 234 views, which I can understand, looking as it does a little like a sample you might supply when undergoing investigations for an intestinal complaint. I keep refreshing and refreshing . . . but no requests.

In the meantime, both children come into the kitchen and announce, as children do, that they really want the noodles/beans/radishes/daal/seeds for dinner, having seen them on the table. My husband keeps asking me, 'Who are these people anyway?' (about the app users, not the children), clearly suspicious and/or convinced that their real intention is to burgle us. It's all becoming quite stressful and still nobody has requested anything. Maybe the pictures aren't flattering enough? Maybe people are put off by the chick emoji next to my name, which I guess indicates I am a newbie rather than only a sharer of Easter-themed food. Or perhaps they are unimpressed by my lack of badges, which you can earn on the app for doing things like reviewing someone or commenting on the forum.

———

Now for some history. Food sharing is one of the oldest types of sharing there is: this makes sense, because food is our life source, so wasting it naturally feels rather uncomfortable, and sharing it surely ensures the health of our 'tribe'. I want to know more, so I get in touch with Clive

Bonsall, Emeritus Professor of Early Prehistory at nearby Edinburgh University, who explains that food sharing was – and is – common practice among hunter-gatherers and important for both group survival and fertility.

He points me to several studies on the topic.[2] In one of these, the authors explore the way that society was organised by hunter-gatherers: into sharing clusters of three to four households within wider residential camps, which varied in size. Because humans evolved a 'dietary niche that often involved the exploitation of difficult-to-acquire foods with highly variable return rates' (which reminds me of feeding my fussy children), human foragers 'faced both day-to-day and more long-term energy deficits', that meant they had to rely on others in their group.

So as humans, we came to depend on each other for energy, acting like a tag team, and social organisation allowed us access to shared food to buffer ourselves against energy shortfalls, as well as to teammates, for better success rates when taking part in cooperative foraging. So not only was food shared, the process of getting our hands on it in the first place was, too.

A second study[3] looked at contemporary hunter-gatherers (the Mbendjele BaYaka in the Congo and the Palanan Agta in the Philippines), and focuses on sharing as a form of insurance against running out of food. 'Foragers

---

2 Networks of Food Sharing Reveal the Functional Significance of Multilevel Sociality in Two Hunter-Gatherer Groups (2016): Mark Dyble, James Thompson, Daniel Smith, Lucio Vinicuis, Ruth Mace, Andrea Bamberg Migliano.

3 Hunter-Gatherer Social Networks and Reproductive Success (2017): Abigail E. Nikhil Chaudhary, Sylvain Viguier, Mark Dyble, James Thompson, Daniel Smith, Gul. D. Salali, Ruth Mace & Andrea Bamberg Migliano.

face resource shortfalls due to three factors: daily hunting and foraging success; illness and disability; and cumulative dependency load . . .' Therefore, cooperative networks which facilitate food sharing are essential to reduce the risk of daily shortfalls. However, shortfalls also occur due to sickness and disease; individuals who are more cooperative, with larger cooperative networks are able to receive essential nutrients when they are unable to produce, buffering them from the negative consequences of failure to produce food over a few days or even a month, and increasing the number of offspring born to mothers.

In other words, food sharing apps aren't just helping us to waste less food: they're making it easier for us to do something that is as old as human society itself, and indeed one of the things that has contributed to its success. That's pretty powerful stuff.

———

Later that day, I spot a little red notification dot on my food sharing app. Fumbling with excitement I jump onto the in-app messages and see not one but five requests, for everything except the noodles (and two requests for the refried beans – who knew?). Ivy wants the radishes and will come by in an hour and Arshan enthusiastically bags the beans, the seeds and the lentils. I barely have time to reply to everyone and make all the typo-laden arrangements necessary when the noodles are requested too. I've done it: every single item gone within a couple of hours.

What will these people be like? Once I've met Ivy and Arshan, will I become so intoxicated by the sense of local community that I never want to stop? It all feels quite personal: someone will be coming to my house and taking my refried beans. Should I dress smartly? Ask them what attracted them to the beans in the first place? Try to find out what they plan to do with them? No wonder I have a chick emoji next to my profile picture. I feel like a complete novice, but rather excited. My family, less so. 'Will they bring food with them for me?' asks my son. No, Jake, that's tomorrow, when I will be, hopefully, on the receiving end, having cleared my schedule so I don't miss out on anything good. Jeff, I'm looking at you.

In the meantime, I list some ready-rolled puff pastry which is careering towards its Use By date. It was bought with some sort of caramelised onion tart in mind, which I don't see happening any time soon. I also download another app that connects people to restaurants, cafés and hotels with leftover food that would otherwise be thrown away. This particular one sells these leftovers in the form of a 'Magic Bag', priced at a fraction of the retail cost. The contents are a surprise, but obviously if, for example, it's from a sushi restaurant, the chances are, it will contain sushi.

I browse the app, which is easy to use and divided into useful sections like 'Recommended', 'Collect Now' and 'Nearby'. Some food you can pick up immediately, some you have to reserve and collect later. I reserve a Magic Bag for the following morning from a hotel on St Andrew Square, which promises to contain breakfast surprises. Jake is off school the next day so I ask him to come and get it with me: we can take our Magic Bag to the garden in the middle of the square and have a breakfast picnic. He's quite excited about the idea, as is the app, which enthusiastically tells me 'You Just Saved A Meal From Being Wasted!'.

Ivy's time slot for the radish collection arrives and I pace nervously by the front door. I want to ask her why she's taking my radishes, but it occurs to me that for people who are picking up only, they're saving a lot of money on food shopping. I get in touch with Tessa Clarke, co-founder of the food sharing app OLIO, and ask her about this. 'People who are struggling hate the stigma attached to food poverty – but with food sharing, nobody is looking over their shoulder. That's why you never hear us talking about people in need. Food sharing is for everyone: the mission is to solve the problem of food waste – and the solution isn't hungry people, because the problem is too big for that. But sadly in every community there are people who are struggling. And the great thing is that food sharing can help. In fact, we often see this cycle, people collect when times are tough; then things get better and they are listing items and giving back again.'

My phone pings and it's Ivy: 'I'm here!'. Are you, Ivy? I can't see you. Then I notice a small woman outside the gate, half obscured by the forsythia, which is in full springtime bloom. She's wearing not only a mask but also sunglasses and a hat, giving the impression of someone under deep cover. Should I have been similarly attired? Will this affect my rating? I don't know what to say. It feels like we should be exchanging the vegetables in a suitcase on a park bench, Cold-War style. I hand her the radishes in a plastic bag. 'Enjoy!' I say, far too loudly. Then, to try to appear less shouty and more normal, I add, 'I hope they're tasty.' Ivy looks at me, I think, or at least looks in my general direction, and whispers 'Thank you'. Then she's gone.

I take Jake to get our Magic Bag from the hotel. The app makes it pretty easy – you swipe your order on arrival and show it to the staff. Calling it a Magic Bag is clever: it's fun and there's none of the stigma that Tessa spoke about: I think it would have felt odd asking for 'cheap food' or 'leftovers', but this seems more like an adventure. The New Town is bathed in spring sunshine and I've brought a blanket, so we take the bag and sit in the grassy area in the centre of St Andrew Square, under a tree. Jake is in teenage food heaven: mini *pains au chocolat*, croissants and blueberry muffins, with little portions of butter and marmalade – and Nutella, as if more chocolate was needed. He takes photos on my phone so he can gloat about it to his sister later. They've even given us coffees – well, a mocha for Jake – and all for just a couple of pounds, with the added warm glow of knowing that if it wasn't for us, this food would have ended up in the bin. Teenagers can be hard to extract from their rooms, but we've not only shared food, we've shared a morning, an experience. We wander home with Nutella smiles.

The following day, determined to get some free food on the other app, I triumphantly secure four chocolate croissants from someone called Kim, one for each of us, to be collected at 2pm in time for an after-school snack. This will definitely raise the profile of food sharing with Phoebe, I decide: she's still wounded from missing out on the Magic Bag expedition. Making the arrangement earns me a 'First pick up' badge. I notice nobody has rated me yet, though. Maybe Kim will give me five stars. Or indeed Louise: by 10am I have also secured her 'Load of Lovely Potatoes' (0.4 miles away), for our evening meal.

2pm arrives and I head off to Kim's, which is a ten-minute walk away. As I'm leaving, my husband asks why I would walk ten minutes to get pastries when the shop on our street, which also sells pastries, is a mere two minutes away. He's not getting this yet. I've also found a used teabag in the food sharing box by the bin. I'm not certain enough that it was him to bring it up yet and, mumbling something about landfill, head off.

Kim lives nearby in Greenhill, a leafy criss-cross of streets lined with tall houses, some of which are divided into flats. The entrances remind me of Parisian apartments, with sideboards and flower arrangements, rather than, for example, children's bikes and a deflated dinghy, which would be more common in my locale. Approaching her gate, I feel uncharacteristically nervous. Maybe this is a set-up, and a terrible crime is about to take place. I silently lament the fact that the last word I said to my husband was 'landfill' and consider phoning him.

I buzz the door as instructed in our message exchange and wonder what to say when she answers. 'It's erm . . . Elle from the erm . . . app.' Amazingly, this suffices. 'I'll be right down', Kim chimes and I wait, half admiring the vestibule antiques and half planning an escape route using the rhododendrons as a springboard into the next garden. But within seconds, Kim appears with the pastries, looking far from murderous and like she does this several times a day. She hands me the pastries: 'They're from Pret, this morning.' At the word 'Pret', I can see myself becoming even more popular with my family. And that's it, Kim disappears, and I am left to walk back home, via Louise's house where she has left the 'lovely' potatoes in a bag on her porch. And they are actually quite lovely, as potatoes go. I stroll along, my bag full of rescued food. It feels rather good, knowing that I have been economical, sustainable, and not kidnapped, all in the space of an hour.

———

I am becoming more experienced at food sharing, although it is not without incident. In the mornings I head to the food sharing app to see what's been listed that I can make use of that day. Some things get snapped up quickly, like pastries, and some things linger for a while. Ella's gravy granules are still there: I feel a bit sorry for them. I collect some Grated Parmesan (unopened) and a 'British Swede' from Joel, which is a good twenty minutes' walk away, but I am fine with that, as it's that time of year when the cherry blossoms are out on the Meadows, and walking down the paths is a pleasure not a chore. I get more Pret pastries from Kim (we chat this time, we have a friend in common, it turns out), and a tin of mandarin segments from Amy, who leaves her offering unceremoniously by her gate. I wait until the street is quiet to take them, in case someone I know walks past, and I am outed on the school mums' WhatsApp group as a canned fruit thief.

When it comes to the listing side, I'm getting used to a daily sweep of the fridge to see if anything is getting close to its Use By date. The sign on the food sharing box by the bin has been vandalised, now reading 'PUT CREDIBLE THINGS IN HERE'. I don't ask who did this, I am just grateful that my family is actually putting things in there at all. I list a packet of burger buns (the barbecue was rained off), a jar of marmalade (I thought it was apricot jam when I bought it), and a packet of bacon (unsmoked), because the shopping delivery brought two in error. The bacon is snapped up by Adam in seconds. I'm starting to get a feel for what goes like hot cakes, which ironically isn't actually hot cakes. Some people show up on time, some a bit late, and a couple of people don't show at all. But everyone is friendly, and apologetic and/or grateful as required.

Later, Joanne messages and tells me she'll be there in an hour to collect the ready-rolled puff pastry, just in time for the Use By date. Joanne clearly plays fast and loose with such things. I head to the fridge to find it, but can't. Am I suffering from Male Refrigerator Blindness? Is it in fact hiding in plain sight, like the mayonnaise often is for my husband? No, it's definitely not there. I feel a rising panic, so rush round the house asking everyone about the pastry. Jake isn't even sure what puff pastry is, my husband is as nonplussed as he has been about anything food-sharing related (although I notice the Pret pastries are certainly not beneath him), but Phoebe sheds light on the issue: she used it for her Girl Guides cooking badge the night before.

I jump in the car and do the least sustainable thing imaginable – drive two miles to a supermarket and buy a replacement roll of pastry. I have two five-star ratings on the app now and I can't risk falling from grace. Back home and flustered, I have only ten minutes before Joanne arrives, and I realise the Use By date on the pastry won't match what was in the pictures I uploaded. Like underage drinkers faking their IDs, Phoebe and I start trying to alter the date with a 2H pencil. Then the doorbell goes. Blushing and over-compensatingly friendly, I bundle the pastry roll at a slightly confused Joanne (pleasant, middle-aged, wearing a cycling helmet), triple-wrapped in carrier bags so she doesn't start to examine it. I feel like I've just robbed someone. But in reality, everyone is happy: Phoebe gets her cooking badge, Joanne gets her pastry (and fresher pastry at that), and I unlock my 7 Day Superstar badge on the food sharing app. It's a proud moment, tinged with sadness as I know that sharing forgery has taken place.

―――

If sharing food is as old as prehistory, what about a more recent example of food sharing in communities? I ask author and historian Alexandra Walsh who tells me about the food sharing roots of a word we use today with a different meaning: dole. 'During the Middle Ages and into the reign of the Tudors, churches had locked, usually oak, dressers known as dole cupboards that were used to store donated food for the poor of the parish who were in need. These food gifts were shared out at the discretion of the parish priest.

'However, the most well-known period of dole is during Tudor Christmas celebrations. The traditional opening to the Tudor Christmas feast was the mince pie. This bears little similarity to the pies we know: it was a mixture of sweet and savoury and was often referred to as a shred pie, as the ingredients were "shredded" together. These were baked in a thick, decorated pastry case known as a coffin. This exterior was rarely eaten with revellers picking out the centre. However, rather than the coffins being wasted, they were shared out to the poor, and this was traditionally known as dole.'[4]

Historian Annie Gray specialises in British food and dining, so I ask her to fill in the gap that brings us up to

―――――――――――――――――――

4 Brewer's Dictionary of Phrase and Fable, Ayto, J., (Revised, 17th edition, Orion 2005); A Tudor Christmas Weir, A., & Clarke, S (Jonathan Cape 2018).

the present day. 'Well, nothing was wasted, so sharing was indeed huge: food that wasn't eaten always went to the poor of the parish (this went on until the 1930s). The way food sharing networks worked within a large house was that a meal would be served to the family, then anything left would be recycled into luncheon or servants' food, any leftovers would be eaten by the top servants, and then anything left from that would go to the poor.'

You see it all the way through history: the concept of 'broken meats and distribution to the poor' was a huge part of royal eating as well. The middle classes did it too, but their food tended to be planned tightly and food for the poor or needy was more likely to be cooked to order (and again, servants ate anything left from family dinners). Further down, in servant-less households – or households with no live-in help, more specifically – you also get sharing. So in working class communities, there's both the 'help thy neighbour' style of things – communities rallying round – and also the simpler shared gleaning or pig-killing scenarios. One person kills their pig, everyone helps process the meat, then everyone shares the stuff that goes off quickly, in a 'pig's fry' – a mix of fried pig's offal.

It seems to me that food sharing in its current 'tech' incarnation is reviving not just what we did as hunter-gatherers, but something more recent, yet somehow forgotten – that's not just about avoiding waste, but about making sure we're all connected and involved, so nobody misses out. This got a bit lost when lifestyles changed, ready-meals and microwaves appeared in almost every home and we became too busy to pop next door with any leftovers, if we even had any, so we just threw them in the bin. And actually, we didn't know our neighbours that well anyway.

Everyone looks like Alexa Chung

There's a shopping centre quite near where I live. It's not a very good one: small and mainly consisting of shops that sell 'everything' – everything being stress balls shaped like breasts and dragon ornaments that double as incense holders: once lit, they give the impression of said dragon blowing smoke. I tend to go there for two reasons: the first being that it houses a large supermarket. The second reason is that it has a Clarks, the shop designed to make you feel like a good parent. It doesn't matter if your children live in their Clarks shoes until they are crushing the children's growing toes. They're 'Clarks fitted', which means you've Done The Right Thing and have a kind of parental diplomatic immunity.

On the way out of the shopping centre is a women's fashion store. It's got the latest looks in the window and is a well-known name. Not long ago it was all Victorian collared blouses and floral maxi dresses for summer parties. When I passed by recently, a puffed sleeve blouse similar to one spotted on Scarlett Johansson seemed to wave from the window. That might look good on me, I couldn't help thinking. And it's only £8.99!

But *why* was it only £8.99? I'm not sure it was for any *good* reason. But I'm human, and having just spent a lot of money and time in Clarks buying children's shoes, I needed a cheer-me-up purchase. So I ignored my inner voice, which was asking me to question why the blouse was only the price of a semi-decent bottle of red wine, and I marched into this famous high street store. And yes, I confess, I bought that puffed sleeve number because it was in *Grazia's* line up of 'Ten Summer Celeb Looks You Can Buy Right Now,' and they had it in a size 14. Plus, it's long enough to tuck in, which is a kind of fashion Holy Grail for anyone over forty. (We don't always tuck things in, we just like to know we could.)

Why did I ignore my inner voice and buy it? Not because I am lazy, or because I don't care, but because I was busy, and the shop was right there, with its summery looking window display and clusters of red beach balls which reminded me of giant haemorrhoids. And because finding an alternative seemed like a hassle, and I wanted instant gratification – even if it comes with that uncomfortable feeling that what I've just bought is probably highly flammable, wouldn't begin to biodegrade for at least a thousand years, and was made by someone younger than my own children.

I also knew deep down that by autumn, when the warm weather was over, the Victoriana look would be *so* last summer. And that the blouse would hide at the back of a drawer for a couple of months, until a Winter Decluttering brought it out again, flimsy looking now. Then, it would go into a bag of clothes 'for the charity shop', which would work its way from the hall to the back of the car. And then, three months later, to that familiar soundtrack of muttering, it would be unceremoniously put in a bin meant for those blue paper towels at the petrol station by my husband as he vacuumed the boot. And the thousand years in landfill would unintentionally begin.

This is how 'fast fashion' gets you. In my head, I'm not that person. I'm sustainable. I wear good quality classics that last from year to year. However, the reality is, I'm just the same as anyone else. I have good intentions and feel a bit choked up when I see that polar bear on the tiny bit of ice (they can swim, right?). But then when it comes to it, it seems too difficult to be a good person when it comes to fashion, just as it is to be less wasteful with food. Like it might involve owning a sewing machine (and working out how to use it) and having what people who wear vintage call an 'eye'. I'm not sure I have an 'eye'. I prefer Zara to have that for me.

———

So what exactly is fast fashion? Thanks to mass production, we can afford to simply discard the clothes we no longer want and replace them quickly with minimal impact on our wallets. As a result, they are designed with a shorter life expectancy and are just not as good quality as they would previously have been. The fashion industry is a huge problem for the planet, with mass production occurring on a scale that is no longer sustainable. In fact, it's responsible for around 10 per cent of global carbon build-up, producing five times more CO_2 than the aviation industry.[5]

---

5 https://unfccc.int/

The 'slow fashion' movement has been addressing this for a while – working to change attitudes towards fast fashion: the cheap 'disposable' clothes just like that blouse. Slow fashion promotes a more sustainable approach, encouraging people to buy second-hand clothes, redesign old clothes, shop from smaller producers and buy quality garments with a longer lifespan.

Which is all well and good, and certainly to be encouraged. But if I only want to wear something a couple of times, and I don't want to buy it new, and I can't be bothered spending days traipsing around thrift shops wondering how everyone else manages to find gorgeous retro pieces in them when I find things from Next . . . then what? Clothes sharing. Yes, that's what. I'm going to wear other people's clothes and let them wear mine (if they want). But what is clothes sharing? It's not quite the same as rental, something we're all familiar with. Even before online platforms and apps, you could easily rent an evening dress or tuxedo, usually from a shop on the high street with soft carpeting and an overpowering scent of peach potpourri. Many such shops still exist, usually used for proms and other black-tie events. But thanks to technology, clothes rental has gone online too, and seen a surge in popularity. These sites, like the shops that preceded them, either own the clothing 'inventory', or stock, themselves, or have it on a consignment basis (on loan from the supplier).

This is still very much in the laudable spirit of 'access over ownership': as a renter, you don't own the item, so one item is worn more often by more people, which the planet no doubt prefers. And it does mean clothing is available in multiple sizes as it doesn't come from someone's personal wardrobe. Clothes sharing is part of the same trend, but not exactly the same, because these apps actually connect you to other people, creating a community and also a greener model in the sense that nothing has been bought specifically for rental purposes. So clothes are only exchanged between individuals, or 'person-to-person'. It's the sharing economy model down to a T: you have a thing, you rent it out – or you want a thing, so you rent it off someone else. And the benefits are (as for food sharing and many other types of sharing economy platforms that I'll explore) the chance to make money, be more sustainable and access things you couldn't before.

These sharing platforms and apps are the ones that I'll be using, with a bit of the more traditional rental thrown in for good measure. And it's worth noting that some of the sharing apps also have inventory available, through partnerships. Which is fine by me: pure peer-to-peer is often difficult for businesses to make money from at the start, and having stock you own is sometimes the best way to maintain quality when it comes to customer service and cleanliness, while peer-to-peer can make it harder to track such things. But this is all a step in the right direction, and I'm here to take that step, in the hope of becoming a more stylish, sustainable version of myself: someone that would pass by that haemorrhoid beach ball shop window, head held high.

———

In the meantime, (and consider this the montage part, if we were watching a film) a gentle flow establishes itself over the next month or so with food sharing, and I'm trying to make sure nothing shareable is thrown out. Clothes-wise, summer is coming, and the social and work events that this presents usually mean one, some or all of the following: a stressful visit to Zara to hastily buy a dress that might magically work for all of the occasions, whether indoor, outdoor, smart or casual; a subsequent visit to Primark having decided I can't possibly wear the same dress five times; an attempt to buy something incredibly hip on Net-A-Porter only to find my debit card is declined; a last-minute call-out on the school mums' WhatsApp group asking if anyone has a dress I can borrow; going to said events feeling both unremarkable and full of self-loathing about the lack of fashion ethics I have, and hiding at the back during any photo calls.

So let's see if clothes sharing can help me – and the planet. The only caveat is that I won't be borrowing clothes to wear around the house. Like most of us, I now have enough joggers and lint-covered sweaters to last a lifetime. But when I go out, I will be wearing something 'shared'. And frankly, I couldn't be more excited to reinvent myself. I start by downloading a couple of clothes sharing apps, some of which look achingly hip and call clothes things like 'pieces' and 'garms', and promise to do things like help you monetise your wardrobe and save the planet. After being initially heartened that the designer clothes aren't the type of oligarch style that wouldn't really suit me (think Louis Vuitton, Gucci and Chanel, *et al*), I immediately get imposter syndrome because I don't recognise the names of most of the 'Popular Brands'.

One is 'Shrimps'. Another is 'The Vampire's Wife'. Another simply 'Goat'. Trying to ignore the fact that everyone in the photos looks like Alexa Chung, I mentally flick through the dresses in my wardrobe and try to think of a single one that was not either £10 in the H&M sale, or ineffectively concealing a large, probably curry-based grease stain somewhere within its folds. Then I spot the word 'Ganni' on the app. I have a Ganni dress! I think I picked it up in a sale online a few years ago. Maybe I am hip enough after all.

The way it works is that you can lend, or rent, or both. Lenders list their items by uploading a few photos and choosing how much they want to rent the item out for. Renters search for items they want and send a request when they like the look of something. Then the two people arrange how the item will be exchanged, whether in person or by post. Apparently, for those who are 'time-poor and wardrobe-heavy' or 'those who require discretion', they offer a wardrobe management service. I feel I require discretion due to the curry stains, but I am fairly sure that's not what they mean.

Next, I have to set up my profile. This is easy when it's all about email addresses and verification codes, but gets distinctly harder when I have to add a photo and 'Tell us a bit about yourself, so your future lenders or renters can get to know you.' They start me off with the suggestion of 'Hello, I'm . . .' I'm what? Clumsy with Indian takeaways? Struggling to find anything in my wardrobe that doesn't scream 'I gave up after child number two'? They even ask for favourite designers. Maybe I could just copy and paste something from the *Grazia* website . . .

I opt for Ganni as my favourite (only) designer and say I live in a smoke-free home with two children, hoping this latter fact will explain the stains and the bad clothing choices. I conclude my intro with something about saving the planet, hoping this will detract from having only one favourite designer, and make me sound like a nice person who knows whether polar bears can swim or not. I am now officially a clothes sharer! First, I decide to rent rather than lend, because the Ganni dress will need some close investigation and a 60°C wash cycle before it can be uploaded. But I am ready to take the plunge.

––––

Like food sharing, and most sharing economy ideas, what clothes sharing is doing is not new: it's an old idea, revived and made easier by technology. So how did clothes get 'shared' before apps? I found out that during the Second World War, rationing of food and goods began in 1940, and to preserve raw materials and factory space for war activities, it was extended to clothing in 1941. Each item of clothing was allocated a points value in addition to money – for example, a dress needed eleven coupons, and a pair of shoes five. To start with, each adult was given 66 points for a year, but over time this number dropped to 24 points, so people had to get creative.

As well as being encouraged to 'Make Do And Mend' by UK Government campaigns, the Women's Voluntary Service (WVS) was set up to help in the aftermath of air raids, and running 'clothing shares' was part of this. Parents could exchange the clothes their children had outgrown and receive points that could be used to spend on other clothes. This isn't dissimilar to my own local network of parents – when a child grows out of a school uniform or coat, it's common practice to post a bagful of hand-me-downs on the local WhatsApp or Facebook group, or sometimes just drop it all round to a neighbour's house when you know they have a child of the right age. Phoebe's clothes have name tapes that peel off to reveal another unknown child's name underneath, and another under that, like old wallpaper revealing a hidden note from a previous homeowner.

I also discover that later in the twentieth century, clothes swap parties (sometimes called 'Swishing') started to evolve as an awareness of recycling grew. Suzanne Agasi, a real estate agent based in San Francisco, founded the self-explanatory 'Clothing Swap' in 1995, based on the idea that 'women reportedly wear 20 per cent of their clothing 80 per cent of the time'. What started as just a few women trading clothes, shoes and accessories in her apartment turned into ticketed events across the country with spa treatments, cocktails, hundreds of attendees – and leftover clothes donated to charities. So it seems what happened both during the war, and here, paved the way for the tech-powered clothes sharing that I'm trying now in the 2020s.

———

By now I'm feeling quite the seasoned food sharer and tell my sister about it when I see her for tea and (free) cake in our garden one afternoon. She thinks I'm talking about leftovers from people's actual plates, which isn't so ridiculous: there was an app in the early days of the sharing economy that let you share your half-eaten sandwich. Funnily enough, this didn't catch on, and I feel like I don't want to know about the incident that led to its downfall. Which leads us neatly to the practicalities. You have to keep an eye on your apps: food comes and goes quickly and exactly the same thing will often never be available again. And on the listing side, you have to be prepared to get multiple requests for an item and put in the time to let everyone who didn't get it know (it's first come first served). I have a prepared, polite 'Sorry, you're too late' message in my phone's Notes folder to copy and paste, otherwise it's time consuming to type this again and again. You also need to make sure you're around for people coming to pick things up – although most are happy with 'It's in a bag by the gate', or 'I had to pop out, it's in the porch – help yourself'. Also remember that collecting things takes up time, but you can usually choose to only see listings that are nearby.

As with all sharing economy platforms, trust between users is vital, so not only are you encouraged to leave reviews, you will be reviewed by everyone who picks up food, to help other users decide if they want to deal with you. I now have a fairly healthy eight reviews, (all five stars so far), and I can also check my 'Impact' in a section on my profile, which tells me how many people I've shared with and how much money I've saved. And because by saving food, we save the water that was used to grow and process that food, it also tells me how many litres of water I've saved.

Food sharing has its pros and cons, like most types of sharing. Let's start with the positives – and the first is a big one: as a family, we are definitely wasting less food. This isn't just because we are listing things on the app. It's also because the act of sharing food has made us (well, mainly me) more conscious of what we are throwing out. Even the children now say, 'Mum, do you want this for the sharing app?' (Or sharing game as they often call it). I'm also doing regular sweeps of the fridge and cupboard, and by looking for things to list, I am more aware of what I have, and what is about to go out of date. Before, my fridge was like a kind of forest of doom: you didn't want to venture too far in as you didn't know what you would find. Now, I am confident that there's nothing in there that I would be ashamed of. OK, maybe not 'confident'. Let's go for 'hopeful'.

I'm being more economical, but it's more than that. Like clothes sharing, it also gives me that warm glow you get from knowing you've done something positive for the planet. But, unlike my experience so far of clothes sharing, I would say it's not quite wrapped up in *such* an enjoyable experience. Don't get me wrong, photographing a wheel of Dairylea triangles is fun, but maybe not glamorous. That said, the free bakery items are great, as are the Magic Bags: there is an element of surprise that the children love, and admittedly, so do I. And I am certainly saving money: partly because I am being less wasteful, so the weekly shop is actually lasting until the end of the week, topped up by shared items. And although I am spending money too, the cost of Magic Bags substitutes what I would pay for the children's snacks anyway.

Another plus: there is a genuine sense of community, and everyone is very friendly, from the app users to the staff in the cafés and restaurants. I even made a friend in Kim of Pret pastry fame and bumped into her at the pub the other night. Meeting people is always interesting to me, so that part of it is definitely a positive. Plus, of course, we're eating food which would otherwise have been thrown away, which contributes to that warm glow.

So what are the negatives? It's a bit of a faff to start with, but that said, you get used to the app and it becomes part of your daily routine to check what's available, and when you're out and about, it's easy to log on and see if there's a Magic Bag up for grabs near you. Once I got the hang of it, it was hard *not* to know what was available and where. However, it does involve effort, and all it takes is one busy day or some unforeseen circumstances and it suddenly feels like it could be a lot easier to just go to the shop. And then there's the food itself. I'm a pretty good cook and I also like a challenge, but there are days when you are faced with some chocolate orange flavour Ambrosia custard and six wholemeal baps, which would be enough to stretch the imagination of even Nigella.

One lunchtime, my husband and I are eating sushi collected the evening before via, of course, a Magic Bag. He munches silently on a California roll and then looks at me, then the assembled spread (which was £4), then back to me again. I feel he's about to say something that's not 'Pass the wasabi'. 'So it would have gone in the bin?' I nod. 'And it only cost you four quid?' I nod again. 'It's pretty good,' he concludes, taking the last piece of nigiri. It is indeed. I say nothing though. Later, I collect another Magic Bag from a nearby French café, just before school pick-up. I am the hero of the day, laden with baguettes, a quiche and some macarons. On the other app, I've scored some free home-grown asparagus for dinner tonight, which Phoebe will undoubtedly pick out of the pasta, but I'm OK with that.

———

My phone, which usually has not much more than a parking app, a banking app and Pokémon *GO* on the home screen (the latter not being anything to do with me) is starting to look quite busy with my food and clothes sharing apps.

One of the clothes sharing apps lists the entire wardrobe (sans smalls, I would imagine) of some minor celebrities. On opening it, I am greeted by Stacey Dooley's somewhat tiny evening dress collection and informed she is 'actively championing' more sustainability in the fashion industry. Would anyone say that about me, I wondered? Or am I just looking for a dress that will fit and costs under £30 for a week?

Under Stacey's smiling visage, a headline on the front page of the app tells me to 'Rent Nanushka, the Hungarian label you need to know'. I click obediently. This particular app is definitely at the *very* stylish end of things, and there are quite a lot of clothes in a size 6, which makes me think that the women who use this app don't necessarily value a hearty breakfast as much as I do: the only thing about me that's a size 6 is my feet. Unsure if I can pull off a Nanushka strapless leather dress on the school run, I head to the 'Just In' section and warm to the app slightly more. The look and feel of it is like a high-end retail site – you might not know it was rental if you stumbled upon it, and you certainly wouldn't know it was peer-to-peer as the clothes aren't generally shown on their owners. I don't feel this will be the app to share my curry-stained Ganni number on, but it might be good to rent something for a low-key event. Like the Met Ball, for example.

I begin planning for some social events: first, an upcoming party. I request rentals from a couple of the apps. With peer-to-peer, because there is (usually) only one item available from the other person, your request doesn't always get accepted, or sometimes when you go into the little calendar to book your item you discover it's blocked out, like a holiday cottage, showing that someone else (or the owner) will have it at that specific time. There isn't as much choice as shopping online but I find a reasonable amount to Favourite on the apps and I also discover that when I go back a few days later, the range has changed, presumably because people are joining and adding more clothes. In other words, the more people share their wardrobes, the more there is to borrow. So, in spite of being a size 14 and unwilling to expose my upper arms or wear neon, it feels like something worth sticking with. It even occurs to me that if I encourage my stylish friends to try it, I will be able to borrow their clothes without having to go on the school mums' WhatsApp group.

––––

The upcoming party is a few weeks away at the home of my friend Julie, and it's the perfect event to try out some shared clothing. I decide to start with a bag, as it feels easier, due to the lack of sizing. I search under 'Edinburgh' to see what I can rent nearby and collect locally. And there it is, an Aspinal of London cross-body bag, going by the name of 'Lottie', that apparently, according to its owner Chantal, although small, 'fits all the essentials'. By the look of Chantal, and from this description, I guess she'd never left the house with a child in tow, but I am fairly sure the bag isn't too young for me and that it will enhance a party outfit no end.

Chantal has provided three pictures, each showing the bag off with a different outfit, and looks like a rather chic but also approachable individual – and she is renting it out for £3 a day. Once I've chosen the dates, I am told how much I've saved already in textile waste and CO_2 (which is apparently the same amount of CO_2 as 44 large lattes). I send my 'request' by way of a friendly message about where I live in the city and wait for Chantal to accept it.

Nothing.

Adrenalin levels high, I refresh the app every five minutes, wondering if Chantal could be eyeing my profile and feeling unimpressed by the fact I only had one favourite designer. Or maybe she's looking at my Instagram (which the app profiles are asked to connect to) and has seen the substandard homemade mince pies I posted at Christmas. After half an hour I imagine this must be what Tinder feels like and I add a rather needy PS: 'Also happy to come to you!' with a smiling emoji – the one with the pink cheeks, which I default to when communicating with anyone under 30.

Still nothing.

While I wait, I request a rental from another app: a dress by Celia B (and rented out by Celia B, which I think must either be an incredible coincidence or just the name the person mainly renting out dresses by this designer uses). No matter: at around £300 retail, it is immediately considerably more expensive and stylish than anything I normally wear to socialise with my friends, but available to rent for four days for £25.

The next morning, I look at my phone to see that Chantal of Aspinal bag fame has replied. I feel a rush of excitement, then disappointment, when I see that she is in fact away from Edinburgh for a few weeks. Maybe she is a student. Anyway, she forgot to update the app with her availability dates and is sorry. Then I notice she has approved and not rejected my request – so the money has been paid to her.

No Chantal, no – how could she? I send her another polite message, pointing out that she's accepted the request, so the money has gone through, and mutter a prayer to the gods of sharing. I need this to work. Within minutes, to my huge relief, Chantal comes good, apologising and refunding the money. Maybe she is new at this too. But the roller-coaster continues: the mysterious Celia B comes back with a bombshell: 'Request declined'. I am at sharing economy rock bottom.

I peruse the apps for alternatives, looking this time in a 'Cult Bags For Under £30' section, and quickly find a gem – a Tara Zadeh (no, I haven't heard of her either) clutch bag in a mustard yellow. It is small and round and feels a bit more 'me' than Chantal's anyway. I decide to make a bold move and rent it for a week from 'Katy C'. Once again, the request is sent, and the excitement begins to build. I amuse myself looking at Tara Zadeh's Instagram and feel both inspired and rather intimidated by this 'Persian Parisian New Yorker' who is also 'Mum of Gabriel'. Her bags are so small, I ponder – if Gabriel is a baby (which he clearly is from the photos), where does she keep the wipes? By the time Chantal has refunded me, Katy C has already accepted my request and I receive an emoji-packed message to tell me that my Tara Zadeh is on the way. I am even now talking like someone who knows fashion by saying 'my Tara Zadeh'. On a roll, I boldly request the same Celia B dress from another app. Accepted! Let the clothes sharing begin.

––––––

So if passing clothes onto other people when you're done with them goes back a while, as we've learned from wartime swapping and post-war swishing – what about the borrowing or lending that's closer to the current sharing economy, where you get your items back? It's been happening in communities for a long time too, especially ones where resources are limited. One of my favourite stories of clothes sharing in the post-war era is from Mark Peterson, who is a sharing economy entrepreneur from the US. Mark lives in Atlanta but his father Joe Peterson, Sr. was born on a farm in 1941, in Gallion, Alabama, in a small community affectionately known as Dish Rag. Mark tells me:

'He was the oldest of seven. And Joe spent most of his non-school time working the land. He was a good student, and had dreams of becoming a psychiatrist, but that would require money and assets. He was also a Hopewell Baptist Church member, a small wood-plank church near Linden, Alabama. One day, after a sermon, he approached the pastor and asked if he could 'Put the Word Out to the Congregation' i.e., let them know of his need for a suit, tie and shoes for a college interview. Most Black households in rural Alabama didn't have electricity in the 1940s, let alone a telephone, so conducted social sharing face-to-face, and if the need was great enough, one could count on the message going 'viral'.

On the Tuesday evening following Joe's Sunday request, an older neighbour came walking down the dirt road leading to the Peterson farm. The gentleman's long stride kicked up dust that would have to be wiped from the suit, shoes and tie he had slung over his shoulder. Joe didn't know him; the gentleman became aware of his request from a friend whose relative attended church.

The suit fitted. The shoes were tight, but Joe could withstand a little agony for the sake of the interview. In a week, he returned the freshly laundered suit to the gentleman – and got a place in college. Social networks and sharing have always been a necessary part of the Black experience in America and have played critical roles in helping African Americans achieve civil rights, pay mortgages . . . and even find a suit.'

———

While I wait for 'my Tara Zadeh' bag to arrive, with the help of my eleven-year-old stylist Phoebe, I am also in the process of listing two dresses for other people to rent. This second part is proving somewhat trickier than choosing something to wear myself. The two dresses in question were purchased BC (Before Children) and also BC (Before COVID-19). The first of these means that my body has changed shape because it grew two humans, and the second means that my body has changed shape because I was stuck in the house for a year eating banana bread. Suffice to say, both dresses are a little on the snug side.

The first, the aforementioned Ganni number with the (now Vanish-ed off) curry stains, is the more forgiving of the two. The other one – a silver-grey bohemian evening dress, purchased in some bygone era when I even had a core to strengthen – won't zip up. But the only people I can get to model it apart from me is one of the children, or my six-foot-two bearded husband. So model it I will have to, even if I can't fasten it. I could stand at an angle, Phoebe suggests.

The photos are taken by Phoebe outside our blue front door. I try to put on an expression that I've noticed seems popular with Instagrammers, where you appear to be pleasantly surprised at something approaching you from the side. The result is more akin to having just discovered an intruder in the shrubbery, and as Phoebe is not adult height, the low angle only adds to my peculiar pose, making me appear to be around seven feet tall and rather jowly. Out of ideas, I decide the pictures will have to do, and upload them to my profile, choosing a rental price that is neither remarkably low nor notably high, so as not to attract too much attention.

To lift my sharing spirits, 'my Tara Zadeh' arrives in a branded drawstring bag, with a card saying 'Thanks for sharing'. The bag itself reminds me of a tiny version of one of the hat boxes my grandmother stored under her dressing table, round and solid, a beautiful shade of mustard-meets-buttercup, and with a strap that my son informs me is 'like the PlayStation logo', consisting as it does of an interlinked triangle, circle and square. I wonder how many of the belongings that I usually carry about I will have to jettison to use it. All I have to do is tap a little button saying 'Received' on the app first, so Katy C knows I have got it safely. Then I am ready.

My Celia B dress arrives too, an olive and blue floral midaxi (a cross between a midi and a maxi, for the uninitiated). The dress is floaty and fits beautifully, as well as being noticeably well-cut compared to my usual high street garms. I feel confident that my PlayStation bag will go with it and start to feel like someone who teams bags with dresses, which is a very new feeling. I remind myself of the other benefits of clothes sharing, and think again about the polar bear, although again I end up just wondering if they can swim, and plan to google this next time I have a minute.

I try on the dress and swing the bag about a bit in front of the mirror. Would I keep it on my wrist at all times, I wonder? Or would my friends think I didn't trust them? Are these the sorts of things fashionable people think about? It's a step into the unknown, like waiting for someone to come and collect my radishes, especially as I am highly likely to spill red wine on either dress, bag or both, being someone that gets quite excited at social events, and quite the arm-waver when relating an anecdote.

I realise I have no idea about the clothes sharing etiquette when it comes to cleaning or, heaven forbid, damage. On further investigation of the small print on some of the clothes sharing websites, I find out another surprising thing about fashion sharing apps: you do not wash the items you borrow, even if you get them dirty. And if you damage them or need to get them cleaned professionally for something wine-related or worse, many of the apps refer you to their recommended eco-friendly cleaning and repair services. A relief, although one tempered by the realisation that my usual organic deodorant will need to be substituted for something a little more reliable, with a fragrance called something like Cool Blue rather than Hemp and Goji Berry. I am willing to make that sacrifice and feel certain my armpits will forgive me in time.

As I swing my bag in front of the mirror, I wonder, has 'access over ownership' overlooked a detail: the joy of owner-ship? Would I love this bag more if it were mine, and nobody else's? I decided that the answer is no. Because – and this is what I am discovering about the world of fashion sharing – the love of possession is replaced somehow, with a love of . . . possibility. And possibility with a conscience at that. Isn't that better than loving a bag that sits on top of your wardrobe for most of the year?

Back on my apps, I plan further rentals. I find a particularly gorgeous dress by Rejina Pyo, as would maybe befit a glamorous Amish woman, if such a person exists. I earmark it for a work event in London a few weeks hence, giddy with the thought of wearing something so beautiful. This is the 'democratisation' that the sharing economy offers: I am able to access something that would previously have been out of my price range. I also Favourite a Ghost dress: summery, bias-cut with a white collar. Nobody, incidentally, has yet asked to rent either Curry Stain or Clever Angle from me, but I am secretly quite happy about that.

The only livestock I like is children

In among the various pages I 'Like' on Facebook, such as the World Economic Forum (highbrow), Edinburgh Live (lowbrow) and Glossier makeup (just 'brow'), sits The Dodo, which is an animal lovers page mainly concerned with sharing videos of brave and adorable rescue dogs, or budgies that make friends with kittens, or dwarf ponies who could barely walk, and 'now they can run!'. The Dodo doesn't even have a 'brow' classification, and even though I'm not a pet owner, I am somehow drawn to it. Especially any videos of dogs being reunited with servicemen who have been overseas. No, *you're* crying.

This is the thing. I like the *idea* of having a pet, particularly a dog. The ones in The Dodo videos always seem personality-packed and goofy, but also obedient. And you never see them poo, which is a big plus for me, as someone who will vigorously wretch over the sink if I have to deal with a 'child treads in dog poo' incident. I'm not sure where my animal ownership indifference comes from.

My late grandmother, the fearsome Mildred, used to declare frequently that 'the only livestock I like is children!'. Maybe I am cut from her cloth, as I would rather cuddle a baby than a puppy, although as a pre-teen, I did have a close bond with my guinea pig Moog: his untimely death was in fact my first brush with the raw fragility of life.

Back to dogs. I have been coming under increasing pressure to join the thousands of people in the UK who have welcomed a furry friend into their household. And although I sometimes see myself as that sort of person, with a happy Labrador at my heels, I'm keenly aware that: owning a puppy is similar to the new-born baby phase (which I've done, and don't care to repeat); puppies cost more than your average holiday these days; rescue dogs often don't like noisy children, of which I have two; I'm not keen on picking up poo; and finally, the elephant (or cockapoo) in the room, which is that owning a pet just isn't that great for the planet.

It's true, I'm afraid. Let's look at the numbers behind it. At a count undertaken in 2018, there were 471 million dogs and 373 million cats worldwide,[6] all of whom have carbon footprints of their own. What they eat annually produces the same carbon emissions as a year's worth of driving 13.6 million cars.[7] And let's not get started on that poo, which I am sure you pick up. But picking it up doesn't mean it vanishes off the face of the earth. The plastic bag goes into landfill, and the poo itself, well, there's a lot of it. In fact, in the US, pets produce the same amount of

---

6 https://www.statista.com/statistics/1044386/dog-and-cat-pet-population-worldwide/

7 https://journals.plos.org/plosone/article?id=10.1371/journal.pone.0181301

poo as 90 million humans, basically a country's worth, so that has to be transported, and processed, with a huge CO_2 output attached. And, as desperate as I am to move on from discussing poo, there's one more thing. You might think that leaving it on the ground is better than it ending up in landfill, but actually, it washes into drains and then imbalances ecosystems in rivers. So . . .

Here's an idea: dog sharing. Maybe, just maybe, there are enough dogs to go round, and we don't all need our own? If there was one dog for several people, maybe there might be a little less poo to deal with? I'm not suggesting people are going to stop owning dogs. But where dog sharing fits in could be to help people who are 'dog curious' like us have the experience, without committing to something which is undoubtedly a big deal, a big cost – and has a big impact on the planet.

So how does it work? Dog sharing platforms use technology to connect dog owners with people who want to look after them (for the experience rather than as a job). Dog sharing has increased in popularity (alongside dog ownership), and there are now several websites where you can do this. There are also plenty of dog sitting platforms, which are a bit different, connecting as they do owners with experienced (paid) dog sitters and walkers. The idea with dog sharing is that there's no need for a dog ever to be home alone, or for people to pay for dog walking or boarding, when there are so many people who love dogs but can't – or won't – have them permanently, or want to get a feel for ownership before they commit. So, in the spirit of disownership, no dog will be purchased by us, for the time being anyway. Instead – let the dog sharing begin.

———

I peruse photographs of 'gentle' Jack Russells and 'affectionate' lurchers on a dog sharing website, and set up my profile. I'm getting quite familiar with the 'upload photo and say a bit about yourself' routine of it. This time, they're not interested in whether I want to eat butterflies, but rather in why I love dogs. Which of course begs the question: do I? I'm not sure yet – I suppose that's what I'm trying to find out. I don't have that many dogs in my life, to be honest. My in-laws have an adequately cute West Highland Terrier that seems to like the children, and licking my husband's face. My friend Annie has an overenthusiastic terrier of another type, which I do not recall, who always thinks I have something more interesting in my handbag than ancient lipsticks, pens and tissues. I wonder if I should cite the tear-inducing Dodo videos on my profile instead . . .

Suddenly 3,000 characters seems a lot. The website tries to help me along by suggesting 'For example, I grew up with dogs, I enjoy spending time outdoors, etc.,' but neither of these is strictly true, unless pub gardens count for the latter? I plump for something about being a 'welcoming family' with 'well-behaved children' who are 'big dog lovers' and 'keen to get to know a dog nearby'. Which really says absolutely nothing about me at all, but maybe that's a good thing. Or perhaps I should mention my deceased guinea pig, Moog. I decide not.

Next I have to say what I'd like to borrow a dog for, but thankfully there's nothing about sharing economy experiments, and it's easy enough to choose for 'Exercise' or 'Company and Playtime' (I pick both). There are a few other box-ticking questions about whether we have a garden or not, and then I get an 'All done!' message with a smiling face. I'm told I can now see 'who is near me' and 'like' dogs. I wonder if they mean 'Like' in a Facebook way, or *actually* like them. I decide to see what's available with four legs in my vicinity. I also wonder briefly if the same people who list their food or clothes on a sharing app, also list their dogs? In other words, is sharing contagious?

My search results appear and excitingly enough, there are lots of dogs nearby. There's Aspen, a Hungarian Wirehaired Vizsla, who 'likes lots of attention' and looks adorable in her photos, like the dogs in The Dodo videos. There's one of her wearing swimming goggles on her head at a hilarious angle, and one mid-leap with her tongue hanging out to the side. Then there's Franklin, a Weimaraner, who is 'great with children' and in one photo wears a red raincoat and a very noble expression. And Frankie, a King Charles Spaniel, who 'is happy to go along with whatever you fancy doing!'. This sounds promising. Maybe I am a dog lover after all.

I enlist Phoebe's help to make a shortlist. She is taken with Laurie, a miniature cockapoo, who 'doesn't really bark' (bonus), along with Ragnor, a Lhasapoo, who 'loves humans and animals alike'. Tosca, a cockapoo, also made it into her top three because of a picture of him wearing a ski jacket in the snow. I wave the list vaguely at my husband, who laughs and asks me who will be picking up the poo. I don't reply, and instead wonder if Laurie is also a dog who 'doesn't really poo', like the Queen.

––––––

The day of Julie's party finally dawns. The summer sunshine that Scotland sometimes delivers is as usual tempered by a cool breeze, but it will be warm enough to sit outside.

Getting ready feels different, with my Celia B dress hanging in its protective bag in the bedroom, staring down at my other, non-sharing economy garms in their usual heap on the floor (my floordrobe, as it's fondly referred to by my family). There isn't the usual last-minute flurry of trying on clothes, finding them to be stained/too tight, or not finding them at all because I gave them to the charity shop, or my husband put them in the bin at the petrol station.

No, I am ready on time, and hardly recognise myself in the dress, holding the PlayStation bag. My husband does an impressive double-take and asks me, rather loadedly, what time I'll be home. I haven't told my friends about the clothes sharing, and feel quite excited about them seeing me in this outfit: it's a far cry from my usual attire at our get-togethers, which generally consists of the Ganni (curry) dress, or jeans-and-a-nice-top, and by nice I mean something from New Look that just about came up alright after a good iron.

Arriving at Julie's, I elicit a whoop from Annie who is first to see me. I try to act nonchalant but end up blushing, a trait I thought I would have grown out of by now. 'Blimey Elle,' shouts Jane from her seat on the patio, '*I'm* usually the best dressed!' Everyone wants to know where the dress is from and the bag is passed round and examined closely. I withhold the sharing bit until I feel everyone is suitably impressed, then drop the bombshell. 'None of it's mine: it all gets sent back next week.' They are amazed, demanding to see the apps. Carol has heard of – and loves – The Vampire's Wife (apparently it's musician Nick Cave's wife, not an actual vampire), and she downloads the app there and then to rent a dress. We haven't even opened the wine and I feel like I am causing quite a sharing stir. I even feel rather pleased with the photos I am reluctantly tagged in on Facebook the next day.

————

As Phoebe and I work on our dog shortlist, more food gets listed, and more clothes arrive. This time a skirt and top, just to mix it up, from another type of site that lets you pay a subscription and rent clothes for a month. It describes itself as like the 'Sisterhood of the Travelling Pants – with each person who rents an item adding life to its story'. I rather like this. The skirt and top feel much more ladylike than I normally wear, and I mull over the footwear issue. Normally a trainer or Birkenstock person, I feel that I need something smarter, but also that I am veering into territory uncharted since the 1990s, when I squeezed my feet into all sorts of bunion-encouraging strappy numbers to go clubbing. Not really a 'shoe person' these days but rising to the challenge for the sake of the sharing economy, I head to the 'footwear' section of one of the apps with some trepidation, but am pleased to find a large range. I find some rather intriguing pale blue sandals by Loq with heels that remind me of little sticks of Blackpool rock. Nothing ventured, I think, and request them for what is forecast to be a sunny week.

I am careful to get as much use as possible from my items and make sure my total spend isn't more than what I would have spent on new clothes anyway. Or shoes, or jewellery for that matter. You can rent a lot more than frocks, I realise, perusing hair bands (the great big ones that make you look like a Tudor lady-in-waiting if you're not careful), belts, scarves and even a scrunchie. I wonder what would make someone rent a designer hair accessory, but then I suppose, if it went with a certain outfit, and you didn't want to buy it, it is no different to borrowing it from a friend, other than the fact that it costs a few pounds to do it.

I go to a book event in the New Town, venturing out of the Southside, swapping turrets and vennels for airy Georgian elegance, which calls for the Ghost dress and Blackpool rock shoes. I keep the latter in my bag, trainers on, until I am nearly there: shoes seem infinitely more damageable than clothes, but I suppose you don't rent something out like that if you don't want to see another person's scuff marks on the sole. Approaching the venue, I pass a boutique I went to a while back. It's gorgeous, all Monsteras and driftwood ladders displaying Danish-designed raffia belts with no prices on. I don't recall the owner being particularly forthcoming during my last visit. Maybe my Birkenstocks and floordrobe attire were not representative of the crowd she is trying to attract. It's still open, so I walk in, more boldly this time round, my sticks of rock loudly clomping on the wooden floor. The same woman is there, and she looks up, beaming at me this time, a vision as I am in Ghost and Loq. I smile, look around briefly, and walk out again, slightly theatrically. I have my *Pretty Woman* moment on behalf of the sharing economy: I just do it in my head. And who needs boutiques that sell £500 sweaters anyway? I can borrow them instead.

———

It doesn't matter that I now have a shortlist of dogs with names like Polly, Aspen and Tosca (well not names *like*, these are their actual names), because it seems that what I do *not* have is the look of a dog lover. To put it more simply, my profile, or attempt at a profile, has alerted the Powers

That Be at the dog sharing website, and I have received an official email. It's from Rosie, who is apparently a 'brand ambassador', and in the email she welcomes me to the platform. This is clearly a smokescreen, as she then goes on to suggest that I 'add a bit more to my description' and recommends that I upload more pictures. Clearly the slightly corporate headshot, indoors and not a dog in sight, is falling short when it comes to inspiring anyone to hand over their four-legged friend.

In the meantime, inconveniently (or should I say sadly) my in-laws' West Highland Terrier Rory passes on. I immediately regret the fact that I never bonded with him which means there are no photographs of me and said terrier in existence. In fact, scrolling through my laptop photos, all 10,557 of them, I am struck by how few there are of me in an outdoor setting at all. Even one of me in a coat would probably help, suggesting that I could go for a walk, because if the situation arose, I would have the right equipment to do so. But no pictures of me with a dog. There is one with a goat in the background at the Cotswold Wildlife Park, but I look concerned rather than happy about the situation.

I decide to find pictures of the children with a dog, and then some pictures of me with the children, creating a kind of connection to a dog, albeit an indirect one. Even this isn't easy. I find one of my stepdaughter and son with Rory but the way he's lying on my in-laws' couch he looks like he's been stunned. Did we take pictures of the dog after it died? I hope not. Finally I find one of the children with what I think might be Rory, but he looks like he has more of a fringe, so I think it might be another dog. And the children look really young, which wouldn't match their ages in my profile description. Maybe I could find some Google images of a dog? Or just walk really close to a dog in the street and try to take a selfie with it?

I go with the one of the stunned dog on the couch, and then another one of me with the children, wearing a coat. Rosie says in her email that 'Owners use pics to help them decide who they think would be a good match for their pup and who to trust so it's really important to pick the right ones.' I'm not entirely sure I have done this. She also signs off 'All the best' which is how I tend to sign off emails to colleagues who are annoying me. It's pretty much code for 'Don't ever email me again'. Rosie's profile picture might be a cockapoo called Alfie but she's actually quite scary, so I hope that the photos suffice and she does not email me again. Feeling more confident, I push the boat out and email the owners of both Laurie and Ragnor, and wait with trepidation for my first canine experience.

Sharing dogs seems so 'now' – but is it? I get in touch with psychologist and author Chris Blazina, who specialises in nature and human-animal interaction, especially the bond with dogs. I ask him about the origins of communal dog ownership, and surprise – like most sharing economy activities – we've in fact been doing it since, well, forever. 'There is still some debate about how canids joined ancient man's fire circle, but the theory goes that more friendly wolves started on the outskirts acting as both scavengers of leftover scraps and eventual protectors,' he explains. 'Friendly wolves over time bred with other friendly wolves helping create the social gene we see in more modern dogs – but they were communal, not just owned by one individual. Later, in ancient Greece, healing temples were dedicated to the demi-god Asklepios who was frequently depicted with a canine companion. At the temples, dogs were shared as healers: those in need had a "sacred" dog assigned to lick their sores and broken parts.

'Other shared ownership examples are found even today among Native Americans. Free-roaming dogs are seen as part of the community and not really owned by anyone. The dogs are usually fed by various community members. By some estimates, 250,000 stray and neglected dogs roam the Navajo Nation, which can be seen as both a community asset and a liability, as wild dogs can attack livestock. The community dog aspects can be seen in other cultures such as in Nepal, where most dogs are free to roam, with a mix of benefits and downsides as they can transmit diseases to both humans and animals.

'The type of communal dog ownership revived by dog sharing platforms and apps seems to be a version of these earlier models, with a first world perspective. It's important to remember that of the estimated 900 million dogs world-wide, under a quarter of them live as pets in developed countries, where we associate dogs with our homes in terms of ownership and a sense of belonging. This new way of sharing dogs evolves this notion of dogs as part of our homes, but doesn't diminish the fact that they are important symbols in our lives.'

———

On the dog sharing website, neither Laurie's owner nor Ragnor's have seen my messages yet. Maybe it's just a slower process, and not like the 'quick draw' sharing of the food apps. Or maybe people are put off by my less than outdoorsy photos, and I need to cast my net a bit wider. After all, Laurie does have 87 Likes, and Ragnor a solid 55. Does that mean that 87 people want to walk Laurie? This is a more competitive environment than I imagined. Perhaps I can't be as choosy. Should I add Benji, who likes chasing birds 'and not coming back' to my shortlist? Or Fredon, who 'likes a good belly scratch' but – oddly – hasn't supplied photos? I go for Priscilla and Trinity (an elderly dog duo – a Papillon and a Chihuahua – who live nearby); Marley, a Jack Russell who 'can be quite wild at times'; and my original favourite Aspen, despite a concerning 252 Likes. With five owners now messaged, I pray that Aspen 'swipes right'.

I show all the sharing apps I've downloaded so far to my stepdaughter Becca. She's in her early twenties and an excellent way to get the opinion of Generation Z. Once I've moved her away from pictures of dachshunds on the dog sharing sites, and noted her genuine confusion at people listing leftover gravy granules on a food sharing app, we head to a clothes sharing app. Becca's generation has grown up with less of a commitment to their belongings and are already using technology to buy second-hand, and 'sell on' stuff when they're tired of it. I tell her it's not the same as the resell apps she's already used to and explain how it works. She mulls this over, and then, as young people do sometimes, gives me a completely new take on it. Instead, she suggests, of paying something off in instalments – you could do this in reverse: buy something more expensive than you usually would, and then rent it out so that it 'pays itself back'. Now *this* is why we have blended families.

I wear a rented dress for a birthday gathering for my niece, prompting confusion from older relatives when I am asked where the dress is from and if it is expensive. My mother wonders why I couldn't have just got something from John Lewis, and assumes I have fallen on hard times, an opinion that is compounded by the fact that I brought some free cakes with me for everyone. My mother-in-law on the other hand can't fathom the idea that I will be returning the dress unwashed. I am actually quite happy about this, as there is a tendency for my husband to adopt a devil-may-care attitude towards washing instructions and I fear returning a dress as a size 8, when it was rented in a size 14.

Some clothes sharing practicalities: first, you have to keep an eye on your apps when renting multiple items and make sure you are organised when it comes to returns. On two occasions, I realised my return day was a Sunday or worse, a bank holiday – but I have also found that a quick message to the owner is usually enough, and most say 'don't worry' or suggest you keep the item longer at no extra charge. This won't always be the case, though, as another rental could be booked.

Returning is fairly easy: obviously it helps if, like me, your post office is nearby. Ideally, as the community grows, it would be good to do more in-person exchanges, as postage (which needs to include insurance) does add to the rental cost. In terms of packaging, I always keep what the item arrives in, and unwrap carefully, so that I can return it just as it came, apart from the added faint whiff of Cool Blue deodorant. Once returned, the owner will review you and you're expected to do the same, both of which will help build up the credibility of your profile and make you look like a trusted sharer. My reviews have started coming in, saying things like 'Amazing share!' and 'Great communication and quick return!', usually accompanied by emojis like clinking champagne flutes and pink hearts. In spite of this, I still only have one 'follower', someone called Eloise, but maybe that is par for the course when you are trying to rent out only two fairly sub-standard items.

Clothes sharing makes me feel I am doing something positive for the planet. But the sustainability part is wrapped up in a very enjoyable experience, so it doesn't seem like hard work. I am now also part of a community: a small one, admittedly, but I can feel that if I stick with it, it will grow. Obviously, unlike some of the free food you can get, you still have to spend money. You could spend a lot, or a lot less. Over the last couple of months, I've spent about the same as what I would have spent anyway on buying clothes. And while you could argue that I have absolutely nothing to show for it, what I like about the sharing economy is that it is, potentially, for everyone. Apps like this could enable someone on a low income to access, for example, a dress for a wedding, or a suit for an interview, that they might not normally be able to afford.

I suppose you have to weigh this part up: would you rather own the clothes, or have the experience? It does take a little adjustment. It's also important to consider that if and when I manage to rent out my own clothes, I can make money back, and even reach a point where I break even, or make a profit. This is the sharing economy dream: rent out, borrow, never spend anything and always have new clothes to wear. I am quite a way off this but maybe I can find more clothes to rent out, and even, as my stepdaughter suggests, buy something for that purpose. On the other hand, not everything that you want is going to be available when you want it: that's the nature of peer-to-peer. And it's also a bit more of a hassle than just buying a garment, because you need to plan out dates and then return the items.

My 'glamorous Amish' dress arrives for a big work event in London, along with a bag by a brand called Staud, which has the look of a see-through shopper with a smaller, crocodile print bag suspended inside it like a Damien Hirst sculpture. This is exactly the kind of thing I would never buy, but is wonderful to carry for a day. Another benefit of the sharing economy to add to my list is the lack of commitment it allows you to have. I like you, strange bag, but do I see this as something long-term? No, I do not.

I get the train to London having clocked a few stares at Waverley station. Do they think I am actually Amish, I wonder? I am hoping the Damien Hirst bag will reassure people that I haven't got lost on the way to a barn-raising. Once I arrive and head to the event in Shoreditch, I feel a little more at home, surrounded as I am by stylish individuals, a description I now aspire to myself. I do notice that rather than looking similarly Pennsylvanian, the younger people seem to favour an Eighties look that someone of my age deeply regrets wearing the first time around, all batwing jumpers and blouson jackets. However, the dress is a hit, and I chalk up a total of three compliments. I would say four but one comment is from the waitress after my fifth appearance at the canapé table, suggesting that the bodice lacing might need loosening. I'm not entirely sure this is a compliment, although it did turn out to be completely correct.

On the train home I flick through recent photos on my phone: Julie's party, my niece's birthday, London . . . I am struck by how many pictures there are of me smiling, and stepping to the front instead of hiding at the back, as I have been doing a bit lately – since children, work, lockdowns and life all got in the way of me being, well, me. This is the benefit I haven't bargained for. Could it be that not buying things has actually made me happier? Maybe, being stylish doesn't necessarily mean owning any stylish clothes.

———

A week or so later, a message pops up on my phone from 'WoofWoof', which I assume to be a dog sharing related alert rather than a message from beyond the grave from Rory. I rush to the site to see who has messaged, willing it to be the evidently very likeable Aspen. But no, it's Marley, the 'wild' Jack Russell. Marjorie, his owner, is looking for extra help as 'the vet students who walk him have exams'. I am immediately concerned that as a person who struggled to even find a picture of herself wearing a coat, I am up against vet students when it comes to the care of Marley, a.k.a. The Wild One.

But nobody else has replied, so Marley it is. Marjorie suggests meeting at Greyfriars Kirkyard, ironically the spot where a dog famously sat on his owner's grave until he died himself. Or something tragic like that. I don't envisage that Marley will ever develop such loyalty for me, but allow myself to imagine a local plaque – nay statue – of me with The Wild One, which tourists come to be photographed next to. I float this idea with my husband who seems to think a tragic ending to this particular chapter is very likely, citing a film about a dog called Marley which I haven't seen. I'm starting to fear for Marley's life and I haven't even met him yet. Or any dog really, for that matter.

But meeting him is proving slightly complicated as every time I email Marjorie on the dog sharing website to arrange said introduction, the message sits with Not Seen Yet By Marjorie next to it, for days. There seems to be an unconfirmed rendezvous at the kirkyard (which is churchyard in Scots, incidentally) the following Saturday at 10am but when the day comes, Marjorie hasn't confirmed yet. Then at 10.05am, she messages 'I am here'. Well, Marjorie, I'm not. I'm in bed watching *Come Dine Champion of Champions* with Phoebe. I feel Marjorie and I have not got off to a great start, but we rearrange, and I hope that Marley isn't aware of this misunderstanding and that he won't take his wildness out on me for my Saturday morning idleness.

You know what they say about buses? Well it's the same for dogs – you wait ages then three come along at once. Next to reply is Alison, dog mother of Priscilla and Trinity, the aforementioned duo. Alison apologises for the delay, but it seems Trinity is having 'up and down days' in her doggie dotage. She also thanks me for 'showing interest in them' which suggests other people don't. Wistfully longing for Aspen and Ragnor, I reply to Alison and arrange to meet her, and secure a new kirkyard appointment with The Wild One. This is how I imagine dating but without the . . . fun? Maybe that will change when I actually have a lead in my hand.

A Germanic beast of a machine

Placed in a situation of extreme peril, for example, a jungle swarming with evil bounty hunters, a zombie apocalypse or a ship overrun by pirates, I have always imagined that I would suddenly (and indeed miraculously, having had no combat training), prove myself to be not only brave, but also pretty kick-ass. You know, doing those moves where you jump up and spin around mid-air, like Lara Croft. Or someone more current – maybe the woman from *Jumanji: Welcome to the Jungle* who was in *Doctor Who?* You get the picture regardless: a kind of warrior queen, unencumbered by the dodgy Couch to 5K Ankle of real life, with the reflexes of a cat, rather than, say, a caterpillar.

This was proved not to be the case at all when, during lockdown, we 'invested' in a VR headset. To the uninitiated, this is a slightly cumbersome eye mask/helmet-type affair, accompanied by hand-held controllers, through which you can play video games that give you the feeling that you are actually there, in the game. I'm not much of a gamer, unlike the rest of the family, and have been known to disgrace myself in *Fortnite* by lingering on the shores of Loot Lake because 'the evening light looks so lovely' and promptly getting killed by someone wearing a unicorn costume. I'm not allowed to play it anymore.

VR is much more immersive than games like *Fortnite* which are just on a screen. I discovered this, along with my sub-standard self-defence skills, when I decided to go in at the deep end with a game about renegade robots. Jake cautioned me but, still believing that my inner Lara Croft was merely waiting in my personal green room eating Hula Hoops and feeling quite bored with my action-free life, I asked him to set me up. A few headset adjustments and a clear space around me later, and I was suddenly on a (virtual) street in a generic US city. It was deeply unnerving, not only because it seemed very real, but because walking past me and around me were seven-foot-tall robots. I was near a shop window where many TV screens were broadcasting a news report warning citizens of a malfunction among domestic robots – these renegades were turning against humans! On cue, as soon as the newsreader announced this, the robots around me, who had previously just been going about their robot business, all turned to look at me and their eyes went red. Then, they started advancing towards me and . . . no, I did not do one of those spinny kicks in the air. I am slightly ashamed to say that, terrified, I yanked off the headset, threw it down on the nearby (real life) sofa and had to go and make a strong cup of tea, post-haste.

And so it went, that the VR has never been used again by me, and is only used a bit by Jake, (who is more of a 'serious' gamer, apparently) and occasionally by Phoebe to do a game which involves hitting cubes of light with virtual sabres. My husband also had a brief VR phase, choosing complex, artistic puzzle games which none of the rest of us really understood but from the outside, it looked like he was grouting tiles in a virtual bathroom. And then the 'Oculus', as it is called, was put away on a shelf, in all its expensive glory, alongside, well, other stuff. Stuff that cost money and then stopped being used. Stuff that had to be manufactured, packaged, distributed and shipped, with carbon being used at every stage. Stuff that we don't really need that often, and that our neighbours probably have too.

———

So, what's with all the stuff? We've got pretty into it, as a species. Having 'things' defines us: our closest living relatives certainly don't need removal vans when they relocate from one part of the forest to another. Chimps use crude tools and make sleeping nests, then abandon them after one use, and most other animals get by without possessions at all. But in the modern world, we have developed an instinct to accumulate more than we need.

This really took off when, in the early twentieth century, a perfect storm took place consisting of a move to mass-production (thanks to factory assembly lines, pioneered by the car industry), modern advertising, and the dawn of consumer credit. Now, a century later, we all have thousands of pounds worth of 'things' in our homes. That's a lot of lamps, radios, clothes dryers, vacuum cleaners, coffee makers, tents, toasters, watering cans . . . oh and VR headsets. Online shopping has made it all a lot easier to get hold of: you can now have a new 'thing' brought to your door the next day or even within hours – and I'm not saying I've never done that (haven't we all?). It meant that even in pandemic times, we could still shop. And we did. Which is a bad thing, right?

Yes – and here's why: we keep throwing it all away. In 2021, 57.4 million tonnes of electronic waste were discarded globally[8] which, to paint a grim picture, actually outweighs the Great Wall of China, the world's heaviest human construction. And this is just electrical items, it's not even all the other 'stuff', like the clothes dryers, tents and watering cans. So what's the solution? Repairing broken items rather than throwing them out can make a huge difference, and repair cafés are becoming more mainstream with that goal in mind, while governments bring in legislation so that consumers have a right to be able to repair what they have purchased. Recycling or reselling rather than just discarding items can also help keep goods in use for longer and mean we send less to landfill.

But you came for the sharing, and I won't disappoint. Because although reselling, recycling, repairing and reusing is all a good idea, how about – just putting it out there – NOT OWNING THE STUFF IN THE FIRST PLACE? (Side note: I get that when we're sharing, *somebody* has to own the item – just not everyone.) So what sort of sharing is this? It's not as easy to define, but I like to call it 'stuff sharing'. These platforms aren't as specialist as food, fashion or dog sharing, for example – which is maybe one of the reasons they've not become as widely used. After all, who do you invite to use a platform or app where you can use it to borrow anything

---

8 https://www.weforum.org/

from recording equipment to bouncy castles, pasta makers to surfboards, and pushchairs to power tools. Does anyone use ALL of these things? Maybe not, but the rise of community sharing on social media during lockdowns has shown that there is a desire to lend, borrow and swap things with our neighbours. And that desire has not gone unnoticed by a new, post-pandemic wave of sharing platforms and apps who are trying to become, yes, you've guessed it, the Airbnb for stuff.

The power drill has become the accidental poster child item of stuff sharing – thanks to a quote (attributed to American futurist Alex Steffen) that did the rounds in around 2006. It said that 'Supposedly, the average power drill is used for somewhere between six and twenty minutes in its entire lifetime. And yet supposedly almost half of all American households own one.' Whether or not this is true, it gets the point across: we buy the drill when what we need is the hole. Which means we buy the pasta maker when what we need is the pasta. And we buy the . . . I could go on, but you get the picture. The point is, it can be a lot easier, cheaper and better for the environment to aim for the result, not the ownership of the item that helps you achieve it.

———

I'm trying out a few stuff sharing platforms, which post-pandemic are popping up everywhere, moving things away from an informal social media group and creating a structured, insured way of getting your hands on things you will need but only for a short period of time. The app I am already using for food sharing has recently launched a section to encourage local communities to share everyday household items like the aforementioned drills, as well as anything from pasta makers to glue guns and leaf blowers, with the aim of helping families both save money and avoid long-term waste. Perfect timing, as I'm already signed up and ready to 'stuff share'.

This is a good place to talk briefly about 'libraries of things', which are another way to share stuff, and deserve a mention, although technically they are not peer-to-peer – and although technology can help them run their inventories, it's not essential. So, are they part of the sharing economy? I'm not sure it matters that much, as they're a brilliant idea, and I'm not that much of a pedant. Often social enterprises, libraries of things (or LoTs) accept donations of the same household goods that people list on sharing platforms. They are stored at a physical location and community members can visit in person to rent out a specific item, just like you would a book from a traditional library. Libraries of things have become more popular in recent economic downturns, and indeed specific types of 'thing libraries' have been around for a long time: toy libraries have apparently existed since the Great Depression; and tool libraries (the first in the UK was founded here in Edinburgh in 2015), have been around in the US since the Second World War.

Back to stuff sharing platforms. I also sign up with one which is specifically aimed at families, because babies and toddlers often require Very Important and Extremely Vital equipment. This equipment – and I speak from experience here – is then very likely to become completely useless the following month, when your baby or toddler can suddenly do the thing that the equipment was helping with. For example, we had a plastic bath seat for Phoebe when she was too small to sit up in the bath. Then, she suddenly learned to sit up and would cry at the mere sight of said item, which cost a million pounds (or possibly slightly less). Suffice to say, family life, and in fact just life, is particularly stuff-packed, expensive and wasteful – as our VR headset would no doubt concur.

With an orange stain on the living room floor, I'm on the hunt for a carpet cleaner, so I browse the 'borrow for free' items in the 'non-food' section of the food sharing app. There's a wallpaper steamer, which is certainly in the right ballpark, and also a copy of *Misogynation* by Laura Bates who is apparently also the bestselling author of *Everyday Sexism*. Is Gabriele, the lender, making a point about me cleaning the carpet as opposed to my husband, who was frankly more likely to have been responsible for the suspiciously sriracha-mayo-coloured stain? I think my concern says more about me than Gabriele, so I move on to 'Listings further afield' and see someone is asking for a Sellotape dispenser, while Jade is offering a cake tin shaped like a skull. There is also a chainsaw available, shown sticking out the back of a van in a slightly ominous fashion. In among the more, shall we say, niche items – a Buzz Wire Drinking Game, a 'funky shape' vegetable peeler and a year's subscription to *Gardeners' World* magazine (how do you borrow that?) – there are actually some pretty useful items, like high chairs, air beds and roof racks. But nothing I need at the moment, and the Electric Churros Maker is 45 miles away. I love neither churros nor the sharing economy enough to drive all the way to Paisley.

I also think about what I could list for other people to borrow. This would be entirely for the benefit of the local community and the planet, as on this particular app you don't make an income from it. My peelers are decidedly un-funky, and my cake tins are shaped like – erm – cakes, but with Phoebe's help I might be able to think of some things. We go through the kitchen cupboard but everything we own seems to have a 'quirk' – like a food processor you have to run for ages because the blade is blunt, or a slow cooker with no hinge that is essentially a health-and-safety hazard. We head to the bedroom instead and find a BaByliss 'Big Hair' electrical hairstyling brush that's in perfect working order apart from the large amount of hair caught up in it, which I then spend twenty minutes pulling out, while at the same time trying to remember when we last had head lice as a family.

On the family-focused platform, where money changes hands, I find a carpet cleaner, a Kärcher no less, belonging to Jenny R and being rented out for £10 a day. It's apparently brilliant at 'bringing carpets back to life' and has a 'low working noise level'. I'm sold. I book it for the following weekend and message Jenny R to arrange collection, feeling like quite the stuff sharing pro. Then, in the Gaming section I find a PlayStation VR headset which, Jake informs me, is different from ours. He wants to try it and also gets quite excited about the idea of renting out our VR headset, as well as another gaming item which I don't really understand with figures and a thing you plug into the TV, called Disney Infinity. He has some other games on disc as well that he thinks might work for sharing, checking of course with me first that he will get to keep '100 per cent of the profit' as he's saving up. I agree, mainly because I am struggling to find anything else in our home that anyone would want to rent out. I am no Jenny R, it seems.

I ask Jake to create 'bundles' of games with similar themes, and immediately wish I hadn't as apparently the games he plays fit into the following categories: First Person Shooter, Zombie Survival and, slightly more reassuringly, Racing. I also notice that most of them seem to have ratings way above his own age and lots of warning signs on the back saying things like 'Bad language' and 'Violence'. Have I been so preoccupied with making sure he gets his five a day that I have overlooked this area of childcare? My husband reassures me that they're 'not that bad' but then I notice the front cover of one which appears to show someone holding a decapitated head up in the air. I tell Jake we can't put this on a family sharing economy site, but he convinces me that the Orc in question is actually holding a helmet. It looks like it has hair to me, but I give him the benefit of the doubt and we upload them, pick random rental amounts like '£10 a month' and then wonder if anyone renting My First Baby Gym and Play Mat will also be interested in playing *Middle-earth: Shadow of Mordor*. At least I know by now that the sharing economy is full of surprises.

Friday afternoon arrives and I put Jenny R's address into Google Maps in preparation for popping out to collect the carpet cleaner, ready for a day of cleaning on Saturday. I haven't noticed the EH postcode is in double digits and I'm slightly alarmed to see it's going to be pretty much a two-hour round trip, traffic depending, as she lives not in the centre but, as my husband puts it, the 'city limits'. He points out that driving to Nutbush would require a section of motorway, which, like renegade robots or outdoor wear, is not really my 'thing'. By which I mean that any more than two lanes of traffic brings me out in a cold sweat. And as much as I want to just get on with it like grandmother Mildred would have done, I find myself accepting the considerate – albeit slightly reluctant – offer from my husband to do the driving instead.

Not knowing how long we'll be, we put the children in the car too, much to their chagrin, having as they generally do a packed schedule of staring at screens. They sit in the back staring at their screens and we set off into the rush hour traffic. Within minutes, we're at temporary traffic lights (4-way Control no less) and the atmosphere in the car turns rapidly from a kind of Dunkirk 'Let's help Mum with her sharing economy thing' spirit to a kind of low-level simmering resentment. As we crawl west through junction after junction, my husband points out that with petrol prices rising, the cost of the carpet cleaner was starting to get closer to the price of ACTUALLY BUYING ONE, so why didn't I JUST DO THAT? He definitely said it in capitals too. Only an hour and forty minutes to go!

Eventually, we arrive in Nutbush (it's not actually called that, by the way, it was a Tina Turner joke that got out of hand) and collect the carpet cleaner. Possibly prompted by our careworn expressions, Jenny R's husband gives us a tip for a shortcut home. But the 'back road' turns out to be so pot-holed it is not unlike one of those off-road Land Rover Experiences that I would never go on, and is a little 'challenging' for our six-year-old Vauxhall Zafira. It is also dark by now, as it's autumn, so to prevent further capital letters I offer to get us all a takeaway when we get home, thus adding further to the rental cost. This is no time for a Magic Bag.

I decide, for now, not to mention the fact that the carpet cleaner is only rented for one day and will need to be taken back to Nutbush tomorrow. Maybe I could get a taxi? Or walk, dragging it by the hose (if indeed it has a hose, I'm not even sure at this point what a carpet cleaner looks like). When we get home I hide in the bathroom and ask Siri how long it would take to walk to Nutbush. A mere three hours and nine minutes. Righty ho. Anyway, for now, it's time for crispy seaweed, the sharing economy's very own olive branch.

———

The next morning, I unpack the box containing the carpet cleaner, which is fairly sizeable, and am immediately concerned by the fact that it contains many, many separate parts and also a booklet as thick as one of my Nigella recipe books. I have possibly misjudged this, as someone who is disinclined to read instructions and even less inclined to put things together. My husband is out for the day with the kids but in any case, all sharing economy goodwill has been used up for the weekend after the drive last night, which he declared to be 'Like going on holiday but without any enjoyment involved whatsoever'. I would argue that the Chinese takeaway was pretty delicious but it's probably better to just let it go for now.

Without reading the instructions, which appear to be mainly in German, I piece together the industrial looking machine in a way that to me looks logical. There is a diagram on the side of the machine itself which helps, although it also suggests I should be using some kind of special carpet cleaning fluid, which I do not have. Twenty-five minutes later, I am able to confirm that none of the neighbouring shops have such a thing either. I contemplate putting in washing-up liquid instead but then remember horror stories of people doing this to their dishwashers and their kitchens turning into an Ibiza-inspired Foam Party. I decide that this isn't how I want the carpet cleaner chapter to end (in divorce), and that I am a practical and adaptable person who will clean the carpets with water, spritzing them with a light eco cleaner as I go. If anyone asks, it's tried and tested by something like *Good Housekeeping* or *Which?* and definitely the 'healthiest' way to do it. And nothing whatsoever to do with my lack of organisation or practical skills.

The carpet cleaner is, in fact, brilliant, a Germanic beast of a machine, and I have – incredibly – put it together correctly. I zoom around, moving furniture like I was born to it and emptying bucket after bucket of grey, fluffy water down the sink. I even get the sriracha mayo stain out. Everything smells fresh and by the time my family returns, I am able to show them that it was a worthwhile two-hour drive: just in time for us to get back in the car and do it again. The next day, once the cleaner has been safely returned to Nutbush, Phoebe throws up – for the first time since she was about four – all over her bedroom carpet. I'd like to say I added this part to be ironic and humorous, but sadly I did not.

———

The following Friday, I book the PlayStation VR headset that Jake had his eye on. Jonny, the owner, responds on the messaging part of the website and we arrange to collect it, and Jake is suitably excited in a teenager-ish sort of way about trying out what appears to me to be exactly the same as what we have anyway. Apparently, however, it's not and I 'just don't get it, OK?'. I am able to smile beatifically at this pubescent grunting because I have just checked on Google Maps and Jonny's house is not two hours away, but a mere twenty minutes, which makes this an immediate improvement on the carpet cleaner experience. Also, with any luck, I won't have to get even remotely involved in setting up this particular item, and nor will it require, to my knowledge, any specific cleaning fluid to be purchased in advance.

Later that day, Phoebe and I eventually meet Marjorie and Marley on Middle Meadow Walk. Despite Phoebe's concerns that we 'won't know what they look like', I spot Marley immediately as he's wearing the same blue coat as his profile pictures. He watches us as we walk over to him and Marjorie, who is elderly, cheery and has a Canadian accent tinged with Scottish. Or maybe the other way around? Phoebe goes uncharacteristically quiet, as children her age do in these situations, and I am forced to greet the dog, not something I would ever do, or indeed know how to do. Marley looks at me, unimpressed, as I pat him and make what I hope is 'dog small talk', complimenting him on his coat and adopting the same slightly high-pitched voice I do when conversing with toddlers. It's as though Marley can see into the depths of my soul and has already worked out that I am not a Dog Person. But he is old, and maybe wise, and something in his expression says that although disappointed, he is willing to give me a chance.

We wander through the Meadows, chatting to Marjorie, who although Scottish originally, lived in Canada for years, and has many adult children over there, as well as lots to talk about. She speaks lovingly of Marley and I find myself glancing at him, warming to his grizzled little face. We sit on a bench and, unprompted, Marley jumps up onto my knee. This is new. Do I play 'Humpty Dumpty', hilariously letting the dog fall before catching him at the last minute? I seem to remember the kids liking this when they were toddlers. I decide that this white-whiskered fellow (or any dog, perhaps) would not appreciate such frivolities, so instead I scratch his back and ears. He gives me a look of quiet approval. Sensing that Phoebe might feel left out, Marjorie tries to encourage Marley onto Phoebe's knee instead, but he stands his ground. With me, there is clearly more work to be done.

———

At the weekend, we drive to Jonny's house to collect the VR headset, a thankfully minor detour on the way to visit my in-laws in the Borders. Jonny's not in but – he assures me via the messaging function on the website – his girlfriend is. After some confusion as there is no number on their house, said girlfriend cheerily opens the door in her dressing gown and a young girl appears behind her. The girl hands Jake (who is wearing a black hoodie and black Ray-Ban style sunglasses, for no apparent reason other than puberty) a large box, looking at him with an understandable mix of confusion and fear. She holds the box as though it contains sacred scrolls, as does Jake, who then chastises me for putting it fairly casually in our boot next to a gigantic bottle of windscreen wash and a bag of clothes that will never be taken to a charity shop.

When we get home later, there is some 'downloading' and 'set up' to do, which apparently I have to get involved in. I don't like to spend longer than about five minutes in my teenage son's bedroom at the best of times, smelling as it does quite strange, and reminiscent of Chinese food, possibly spring rolls, even when we've not recently eaten Chinese food. My friends who also have teenage boys assure me that it could be a lot worse. Anyway, after some inevitable outbursts about how terrible our Wi-Fi is (it isn't), and how there are bits missing from the box (there aren't), he starts playing with the VR and I am thankfully no longer required. But for some reason I am now craving Won Ton.

My mother calls in for a cup of tea and I tell her what Jake is doing. She doesn't want to try the VR as it 'could make her dizzy', which I'm quite glad about as instead she tells me stories of doing exactly this kind of community sharing of domestic 'stuff' during her childhood in the Cotswolds in the 1940s and 1950s. Her grandfather, my great-grandfather, was a baker, and had a huge oven, similar to the ones you see in pizza restaurants, which need a special spade-like tool called a peel to get the bread in and out. 'It was the late 1940s and not many of the local women would have had an electric oven, or if they did it wouldn't have been big enough for a large joint of meat,' she tells me.

'I remember clearly, on Christmas Day, my grandfather would have the bread oven on, it was always on I think, and the local women would come round with big tins containing their Christmas roasts, tied up with string and surrounded by potatoes. There would be beef, pork, capons, the occasional goose. All the tins looked different, and throughout the morning I'd watch as my grandfather would open the oven to baste them one by one. The smell and the sizzling sound made me so hungry! Then at 1 o'clock on the dot, the door to the bakehouse would open again and all the women would be waiting, lined up and clutching big cloths. He'd pull out the tins, hand the right one to each woman (he never got this wrong), and then they would wrap their roasts in the cloths and run off up the road in their aprons to their awaiting families.

'When I was a bit older, the Queen was crowned and we were all desperate to watch the event. The only problem was that we didn't have a TV yet. Quite a few people we knew bought a TV just for the coronation. I was hoping we would too but we didn't, maybe we couldn't afford it, so instead we had to go round to one of the neighbours to 'share' theirs. There was only one channel: not like these days, it was just the BBC then. And that day it was on for much longer than usual, on 'normal' days the schedule was only a few hours in the afternoon and then again during the evening.

'Our TV-owning neighbours, Darrell and Elsie, had a living room just like ours – everyone did, it wasn't like today when everyone tries to have a different style. There was a tiled floor with a big patterned rug, and in the fireplace was a 'range', like a burner: the only heating in the house with a little oven on the side. Not many people had new furniture so it was all from before the war, dark wood sideboards and uncomfortable sofas. In the corner of the room was a tall, varnished, wooden unit, like a chest, with double doors at the front. That was the TV – the doors would be folded back when you watched it and then closed again, so it looked like a piece of furniture.

'The day of the coronation, the doors of the unit would have been opened early and the tuning signal would have been on for an hour or so, allowing Darrell to make sure the picture was as clear as possible. The live coverage started at about 11 o'clock in the morning and I remember we went round after lunch, which I'd had earlier than usual that day: a fish paste sandwich. There were already about six or seven other neighbours in the room when we got there: adults sitting on chairs – some of them would have brought their own. The children were sitting cross-legged on the rug, and my brother and I joined them. It was uncomfortable but we had the best seats in the house: the TV screen was tiny and curved so the picture was hard to see. Elsie gave us a lemonade and we knew we would have to make it last. When the Queen stepped out of the carriage at Westminster Abbey with her bouquet, like a bride, I just couldn't believe that what I was seeing was actually happening in London right that second. It felt like magic.'

Jonny and his girlfriend are our very own Elsie and Darrell, and Jake plays with modern magic, their VR, for most of the weekend – except when forced by me and my husband to 'do something useful' or 'get some fresh air'. It's a vaguely worthwhile experiment – he wants to get a PlayStation VR and this gives him a chance to try it out, so that if he did save up for one, he'd know what it was like. This is an underrated benefit of the sharing economy: quite often our unnecessary purchases are based on the fact that we think we want something when in fact we might not. And in this case, that proves to be true: Jake enjoys marching about his room shouting about Iron Man and waving two hand controllers that look like lollipops, but by the time we pack the whole thing up on Monday to take it back to Jonny, he decides it isn't as good as our own. And, grudgingly, he admits it has been sensible to try it out. I even get a hug.

———

Phoebe and I start walking Marley every week, on a Friday afternoon. Marjorie lives in a retirement flat about ten minutes away from us, and on her front door she has a sign which says 'Beware of the Jack Russell', and a Jack Russell themed front door mat with 'Welcome!' in a speech bubble coming out of a Jack Russell's mouth. There's also another sign with the word 'Marley' on it and lots of other, smaller words around it like 'Vocal' and 'Fearless'. It doesn't quite match the quite statesmanlike dog that we're getting to know: maybe these were bought when he was younger.

To start with, Phoebe and I don't really know what we're doing, and bicker gently to each other about the length of the lead and whether or not to let him stop and sniff whatever it is he wants to sniff. Marjorie has told us he doesn't like other dogs and sometimes it's just best to pick him up if he starts getting aggressive. I pray this won't happen, and pray also that he won't poo when we're with him, although she does give us a Mister Man themed poo bag dispenser every time we collect him, which Phoebe loves, and I feel slightly unsure about. As we walk along, I'm amazed at how much attention he gets, much more than when I used to push a buggy with a baby in it. Or maybe I was just too tired to notice back then. Marley loves the attention and smiles rakishly as strangers pet him, dapper in his blue bandana. Do dogs smile? Can they look 'rakish'? I'm beginning to wonder what's happening to me.

Marley is starting to look pleased to see us when we pick him up. The following week we walk him along past our house. He's not keen, this isn't his usual route, and it's also raining, and the pavements are sludgy with autumn leaves, which he doesn't seem that happy about. Nonetheless, I bring him in to meet my husband who is rather taken with him, being a Dog Person. Marley sits on my husband's foot and looks at me as if to question why he would go back out in the rain again and not stay with this man who knows exactly how to scratch his ears. We stay for a while, and Marley makes himself at home. As Phoebe and I leave, I hear my husband mutter that he's a 'good wee dug'. We head back to Marjorie's, the lead wrapping itself around our amateur dog walking ankles, as it always does. But Marley is patient, lifting his leg obligingly when we untangle him.

We are nearly at Marjorie's when Marley stops suddenly and adopts a stance that fills me with dread. The time has come: poo time. The street is busy and once the gift has been delivered, and Phoebe and I have exchanged looks of panic, I feel I have to act quickly just in case anyone thinks I am going to leave said gift there on the pavement. I scramble for the Mister Men dispenser and pull a poo bag out. The bag looks quite small and thin: I was hoping for more of a bin liner so I could be sure of no contact at all with the poo. But this is what I have to work with, so work with it I must, and seconds later I have a warm dog turd in my hand, separated from my skin by a millimetre of black plastic. This is, for me, the stuff of nightmares, and to make it worse, there are suddenly no bins in the entire world, so I have to walk with this tepid terrier offering in my hand for the length of an entire street before I am able to dispose of it. They say that when it's your own dog, it's like changing a baby's nappy: you don't mind. Well Marley is not my dog, I am merely sharing him, and I'm not going to lie, I do mind. I can't really look at my right hand for the rest of the day, even after I wash it very thoroughly, several times. It's like the actual opposite of shaking hands with a celebrity and never wanting to wash your hand again.

This week we meet Alison too, who brings Priscilla, the Papillon, not Trinity, the latter being 'poorly'. They're both very elderly, Alison tells us, and she doesn't know how old exactly as she inherited them both from a neighbour of hers. Priscilla is not dissimilar in size to my childhood guinea pig Moog and I'm struggling to find a space to stroke her that's large enough for my hand. She limps, and also has a kind of growth on her nose which although unfortunate is also similar in size and shape to her actual nose, creating a kind of two-nose look. I'm sure she's a lovely old lady but there is something of the rodent about her, and Alison confirms this when she tells me that greyhounds often chase her thinking that she's a 'lure'. I have to google that word later: it's the name for what greyhounds chase when racing on a track, like a fake rabbit.

Alison is in her fifties, I estimate, and chatty although a little melancholy. She hasn't long been in Edinburgh, having moved here from the south of England after her husband died. I think she's lonely, and catch a tear sliding down her cheek at one point. I hope Priscilla and Trinity are good companions for her. She doesn't ask us to walk them again, and I wonder if one, or both of them, have died. I look out for Alison on the Meadows sometimes when I walk Marley, her little lures on leads and a tear on her cheek, but we never see her again.

Please wait to be seated

When you have small children, as I used to not that long ago, it's amazing what can be dressed up as an 'activity'. Something that not only satisfies the children themselves, and makes them feel like they have done something with the rainy Tuesday morning in question, but also makes you feel like you have performed adequately as a mother. 'What are we doing today Mummy?' We're going on an adventure – to the doctor's! To the library! To the post office! To the carwash! If it can be strung out for longer than thirty minutes, it counts as An Activity, and therefore we can Tell Daddy About It Later, and perhaps a picture can be painted documenting the experience, which will then be attached to the fridge. One such 'activity' is 'Going To IKEA!'. In fact, it's pretty much the gold standard of such activities. You get to buy a packet of teaspoons, a bath mat and a bag of mini Daim bars – the children get to run around the pretend bedrooms for an hour. It's a win-win, as long as nobody gets lost, like the child found living in an IKEA store in China for six days, although I'm fairly sure this was intentional.

So we all love IKEA. And indeed what's not to love? Tealights, meatballs, the disquieting feeling that your child might actually use one of the display toilets in the fake bathrooms. And of course furniture, which is in many cases as cheap as the proverbial chips. Bedside table for a tenner? Don't mind if I do. Wall shelves for seven quid? A lick of paint and nobody will know. A kitchen chair for £12? Thank you kindly. And because they all have titter-inducing Scandi names like Knutstorp, Flärdfull and Smörboll, we feel all European and stylish about our bargain hunting, go home to eat our Daim bars and feel slightly smug, if not a little 'hygge' about the whole thing. Although I think that's Danish, not Swedish.

But *why* is the chair only £12? Just like the puff sleeved top, I'm pretty sure it's not for any particularly good reason, and I'm almost certain that said item was neither hand crafted from sustainable timber nor built so that it can be passed down the Tucker generations, an enduring memory of life in the 2020s. But I have two small children (or did, now they're all hormones and Snapchat notifications, but similarly time-consuming), and I need a bedside table/shelf/chair without either remortgaging or going to too much effort. It's that instant gratification all over again.

But that's not to say I haven't tried doing it the 'other' way. In lockdown, a chest of drawers appeared on the pavement outside our front gate, probably awaiting uplift by the council. I called out, at a safe distance of two metres of course, to the neighbour leaving it there and asked if I could have it, then dragged it inside. It was old, probably about seventy or eighty years: 'Late Hitler' as my father would have called it. He knew his antiques; me, not so much, and

I proceeded to disfigure it using the 'shabby chic' method. Hours were spent in the back garden layering on Farrow & Ball paint in a shade called something like Otter's Testicle, only to then try to remove said paint artfully from the edges of the drawers with sandpaper and a chisel (OK teaspoon), to give it that lived-in look. The result was less lived in and more died in, and as much as I scrubbed the inside of the drawers and lined them with Cath Kidston scented paper, the mould prevailed and Phoebe refused to store her socks in it because it 'smelled of Parmesan'. I arranged a council pick-up for the chest of drawers shortly afterwards.

But I still see myself as *that* person, somehow. Searching for junk shop finds, doing them up with a dab of Otter's Testicle and a teaspoon and having everyone marvel at how I manage to juggle the kids and work with all the wonderful upcycling I do. But the reality is, I'm the woman in the queue at IKEA who only came in for six wine glasses and now has one of those extra-large trolleys without the sides that they give to people who have an IKEA Family Card. (Since you ask, yes I do.) But I also have good intentions when it comes to my interior design. I don't want to buy fast furniture any more than I want to buy fast fashion. I want quality things, made thoughtfully, that last, but without spending thousands of pounds. By which I mean I don't have thousands of pounds to spend. And I emphatically don't want to try the upcycling thing again, because, well, I've got a book to write.

———

Fast furniture is the phrase coined for the cheap, borderline disposable interior design made popular by those on the hunt for a bargain, those renting and moving frequently – as well as people after a quick update to the look of their home in line with décor trends which, often thanks to social media, now change as frequently as clothing fashions. It's so cheap that quite often it makes more financial sense when you're done with it or moving house to throw it into a skip than pay for a removal van, and then just start again when you get the keys to the new place. The problem is that fast furniture is as bad as fast fashion. In Britain alone, people get rid of more than 300,000 tonnes of reusable furniture every year – and a third of UK adults throw away furniture that could be recycled or reused. Not much *is* recycled, because while clothing is made of (unsurprisingly) mainly cloth, furniture is made of loads of different materials, like wood, metal, glass, fabric, leather . . . And in the case of that kitchen chair, of course, plastic.

This disposable attitude towards furniture is relatively new, and the increase in furniture waste far exceeds population growth over the last half century. Just like the fashion industry, the environmental problem with 'fastness' when it comes to furniture sits alongside ethical issues. Much of the manufacturing goes on in countries where lower wages can be paid and this, combined with cheaper materials, flat-packed shipping and 'build it yourself' design, means that furniture is cheaper than it's ever been.

The slow furniture movement campaigns to reduce waste by encouraging us to buy better quality interior design, shop locally, upcycle (one word: Parmesan) and to recycle or dispose of our furniture responsibly when we do need to get rid of it. Sounds like a plan, but it also sounds like it could be expensive and/or time consuming. I mean, I'd love to be in a position to commission a local craftsman to build me a bespoke cabinet for my living room from nearby trees, which were then immediately replaced by more lovely trees – but the fact is, if I had twenty grand in loose change in my purse I'd probably be writing this on the Amalfi Coast. But I'm not, I'm at my kitchen table in Edinburgh. And it's raining.

A word about IKEA here. In spite of using them as an example of fast furniture, they have been working hard to change some of their practices, such as making commitments when it comes to renewable energy, and introducing a new buyback service which lets customers return old furniture and get a voucher worth up to half of the item's original value. The returned furniture will then be resold to a new home, giving it 'a second chance at life'. I can honestly say that after a few years in my home, nobody would want anything I took back, but IKEA claims the scheme will reduce waste and increase sustainability. They are also promising more spare parts to help people repair its products. And finally, there is an argument that the 'particle board' (a mixture of wood chips and glue) that is the lighter and less durable version of wood used to make their furniture means that less 'real' wood is used and the wood that is used is often actually leftover wood scraps, so fewer trees will be cut down.

So what's an eco-worrier like me supposed to do? Yes, you've guessed it, there is now a way to share your furniture – although it is a branch of the sharing economy family tree that's not that well known. But 'disownership' of furniture is becoming more popular, thanks in part to social media (our rooms need to be Instagrammable – and constantly changing – these days), and sustainability. But there's another reason: because of the rising cost of living, student debt, delayed marriages, frequent job hopping and a focus on experiences over possessions, people are drifting further away from furniture ownership. Everything – as we've all discovered recently – can suddenly change: so why buy permanent, expensive items when we don't know what our lives will look like a year or two from now?

With an imminent house move on the agenda for us, the timing couldn't be better to try some furniture sharing. But first, let's talk about the word sharing here, because once again there is a difference between 'sharing' and 'rental'. Furniture renting has actually been around for a while, just like the kind of high street clothes rental we spoke about before. I ask Lennox Cato, who is an *Antiques Roadshow* furniture specialist, about this (I don't know him, but I track him down in his antique shop and he is very forthcoming). He tells me that during the post-war period particularly, the norm, especially for the working classes, became the renting of furniture and domestic appliances which were included in the rental of your home, in the same way a 'furnished let' works today. It wasn't always possible to afford the things needed to make homes pleasant to live in, which is why renting them made sense. Technology has taken this out of the landlords' hands and allowed furniture rental platforms to spring up, particularly in the US (which has longer distances for removal vans to drive). Some of these offer a complete 'white glove' service of furniture delivery, set up – and removal when you leave your rented home for the next one.

Furniture sharing, like clothes sharing, is all about having a thing and renting it out, or wanting a thing and renting it instead of buying it. In the world of home interiors, doing this has huge green credentials, as furniture is a big thing to put in landfill, and there's a lot of it going in. It also means you can have things in your home you wouldn't normally be able to afford, or tap into interior design trends temporarily without wasting money. Most of these websites are at an early stage and some offer a mix of the aforementioned rental (various brands list what they have for people to rent instead of buy), and pure peer-to-peer, which means individuals listing homeware items that may be in storage or are not often used. It's all change, and my plan is to see what's available and give it a try. Our new home will contain neither a Knutstorp, a Flärdfull or a Smörboll, and no Allen key will be used in the restyling of our new living room.

———

We're only moving to the other side of the Meadows. Most places look the same in this area: it's all flats (ours is a ground floor, so has its own front door and garden) with big rooms, corniced high ceilings, small, narrow bathrooms, and usually the odd mouse. Anyone who's lived in Edinburgh will also know about the 'Edinburgh press', a door-shaped open cupboard in every sitting room in these tenements, which provided access to builders across all the flats in the block as they were being constructed. The 'presses' were closed off and turned into shelves when the flats were completed. I could tenuously relate this back to sharing by saying it was about 'shared access' but the truth is, I just think it's interesting.

We clear out the place we've lived in for six years, putting furniture we don't want any more out on the pavement with a sign saying 'HELP YOURSELF', and I also list some items on the local Facebook group, The Meadows Share. It's an odd place, this group, where someone once listed ice cream that was melting – you had to get to Marchmont Crescent in the next ten minutes, realistically, they said. There are also a lot of rooms to rent, lost cats, and the occasional takeaway that's gone to the wrong house. The other day someone wanted an 'extra large' magnet but was unclear why. My IKEA cast-offs get snapped up, though, along with bag upon bag of clothes (mainly Jake's and Phoebe's) and some toys. Predictably, every time I put a bag of toys out to be picked up and post a photo on the Facebook group, Phoebe decides she doesn't want to part with the contents. We have one last nostalgic play with the Playmobil, which involves me trying to make the Modern Luxury Mansion even though many of the pieces are missing, and Jake wanting to introduce a serial killer related storyline to the game. After this short-lived attempt to step back in time (in which a fairy, a pirate and a cow sadly lost their lives) the overflowing bag of miniature German people and animals goes out by the gate along with a GLADOM (a small table to you and me) and a TROTTEN (a pretty ugly white desk), to be collected by someone called Debbie. I borrow a lawnmower for two hours from someone on the next street called Graeme, using the 'non-food' section of the food sharing app, and my husband mows the buttercups. The council picks up two battered armchairs, and finally, the decluttering is complete. Now, it's time to rent.

I register on a furniture rental website, which is fairly successful, aside from an initial issue where predictive text, for some inexplicable reason, creates my profile name as 'Electric Turkey', as if that is something I type more often than my ACTUAL NAME. Once this is resolved, I'm pleased to find that it doesn't feel any different to a 'normal' furniture website where the items are being sold, albeit there are slightly fewer things listed. In the new place, we've got a few gaps to fill, and these are things I'd normally buy, so renting them feels exciting and as though I can choose things I wouldn't normally. My husband is anxious about the inevitable wear and tear that we (and by 'we' he means the children) will inflict on the chosen items, but I reassure him that according to the platform, 'Life happens!'. He feels this is a little vague so I elaborate and tell him that apparently they can get most stains out themselves, 'to make the furniture look as-good-as-new'. More ominously, for extensive damages, we have to contact them to 'evaluate next steps'. So this means Phoebe, who has a reputation for spillage, will not be allowed near anything we rent with any form of food or drink, Magic Bag contents or otherwise. Shared food doesn't stain any less, and I don't want to have to drive to Nutbush again. I mull over whether a carpet cleaner would even work on furniture and hope I don't have to find out.

Another area of concern is that the removal men are booked, the packing has begun, and we will have hardly any seating in the new place unless I get renting sharpish. Again, I am reassured by the fact that the website tells me that my new furniture (or maybe fashionable people call it 'furns', like garms?) will be with me in a mere two weeks. This is already more appealing than buying, as many furniture retail websites are quoting not weeks but months for delivery at the moment, probably because of lockdowns/

inflation/the world just going a bit wrong in general, so it seems preferable in every way – and appeases my husband who doesn't want to sit in Jake's gaming chair of an evening for the next six months.

I find a table to replace GLADOM, called the Agra which boasts 'intricate carving' and is only a couple of pounds a month, an ottoman (which I've wanted for ages but haven't really been able to justify) in a kind of moss green, and two leather armchairs, which I'm very excited about. I love leather armchairs, from the smell of them to the look, and these are beautiful, and retail at a grand a piece. They have a bit of stitching detail and are described as an 'unusual take on a classic design'. SOLD. (Well, rented.) I put my order in, feeling a sense of disbelief that for so little cash, all this furniture will be turning up at the door in a matter of days. Could it really be this easy?

––––

Middle-earth: Shadow of Mordor and the other equally inappropriate PlayStation games don't exactly fly off the virtual shelves, as it were. In fact, much to Jake's irritation, he gets precisely zero requests for them – so his savings fund doesn't get the boost he had hoped for, and instead continues to be depleted by essential purchases such as more black hoodies and what I erroneously refer to as 'Dungeons and Dragons toys' (apparently the word is 'figurines'). This is the way of stuff sharing: it seems some things will be very popular, some things won't. I think an item has to be of a high enough value that it would make a real difference to not buy it, and it would also need to be something you need infrequently enough so that a large outlay would not feel like an investment. That's maybe the difference between a carpet cleaner and the Disney Infinity thingy.

The upside of this is of course that by using a stuff sharing platform, I have access to things I wouldn't choose to own, or indeed store. Because, to use the carpet cleaner as an example again, it – just like baby equipment, tents, kayaks, lawnmowers etc – is huge, and another feature of Edinburgh city living is that storage space is not generous. We keep, for this reason, a lot of 'large items' (by which I mean boxes of crap) in my mother's garage, as she lives a bit further out of town, where garages are actually a thing. So there's another advantage: stuff takes up space, and not all of us have much of that. (And space can also be shared, which we'll talk about a bit later on.)

As well as this, furniture sharing gives me the rather pleasing feeling once again that I'm doing something not just differently, but more positively. Admittedly, it's not wrapped up quite as elegantly as fashion sharing, but Jake might disagree. What else? The people I've dealt with have all been very friendly, and I could see that if you used platforms like this regularly enough, you would certainly feel part of your local community. Stuff sharing platforms – unlike clothing rental, where it's easier to put the item in the post – tend to operate locally, and as I discovered through bitter experience, the minute you start driving long distances to get something, you negate the benefits quite quickly. And the love of your family.

What about the cons? To be honest, they are few and far between. You might not find exactly what you want for when you want it on a platform but the more people use them, and the more people list, the sooner we can create communities locally who make money from what they own, and rent their neighbours' stuff rather than buying it. And unlike fashion, there isn't that 'Will it fit?' or 'Will it suit me?' concern. A hedge trimmer is a hedge trimmer, and if you don't like the fact that it's orange or says 'Black & Decker' on it, then maybe you should get someone else to trim your hedge. (I say this as someone who has little experience of hedges and/or hedge trimmers.)

The fact is, I could get into this type of sharing, and I think I will: I've just scratched the surface but the more I think about it, the less stuff I want filling up my cupboards and Edinburgh presses. And I don't feel an attachment to things that have a plug, apart from maybe my hairdryer. It feels quite freeing, quite Marie Kondo, quite joy-sparking not to own a bell tent, or a pizza oven, but just to know that they are out there, nearby, available and currently being used and enjoyed by many people in the local community, just like that TV was all those years ago on Coronation Day.

———

The rented furniture arrives in various batches, which makes sense because the website is a marketplace which means it offers furniture and interior design from various different individuals, designers and manufacturers, all in one place. So, it's a bit like Etsy or eBay but you're not renting and not buying. My choices were 'mixed', to be kind to myself. The Agra table looks like it would fit in well in the 'Please wait here to be seated' area of the nearby Middle Eastern restaurant, but nobody in the family appears to hate it, so I stick it in the hall with a candle and a plant which doesn't need much light on it, and decide to reassess it at a later date. The ottoman arrives a few days later, somewhat dramatically. On hearing the doorbell, I walk from the kitchen to the front door along the hall, and a large tabby cat passes me, walking in the opposite direction, barely glancing at me – as if this is its daily commute and who the hell am I to question it? I stare at it, bewildered. How much coffee did I have this morning? We don't have a cat. I don't even like cats that much, although I do rather admire their attitude.

I open the door to the man delivering the ottoman and shout 'WE DON'T EVEN HAVE A CAT' at him. He appears alarmed, probably because by this time the cat, which might provide some context for my outburst, has now disappeared round the corner of our new, 'T' shaped hall. He hastily puts the box down in the porch and backs off, maybe wondering if there is such a thing as a crazy *non*-cat lady. Once he's gone, I shut the front door before turning to chase after the gigantic, completely unphased feline which is now standing looking quite disdainfully at the Agra table. Maybe it isn't a fan of meze. Eventually I persuade the unapologetic animal, who must have come through the French doors in the kitchen, to take the same route back out again and stop judging my rented furniture. Wondering what it means if even cats don't like my table, I unwrap the ottoman, and am immediately cheered by this joyous green velvety number with screw-on mid-century style legs. Scowl at those, moggy.

The leather chairs, which I am most excited about, turn up a day or so later when I'm out walking Marley. I get a cryptic WhatsApp from my husband: 'Chairs are here. Perfect for when we have nursery age kids again'. I wonder what he means. That they're practical, and wipe clean? That they have character, which would appeal to young children? I feel I'm clutching at straws here because I have a sinking feeling that what he means is that they are small. I reply by asking him that very question, praying to the gods of sharing that they are not comedy chairs but gorgeous, giant, welcoming, snuggle-up-in leather chairs. By now, Marley is getting irritated with me stopping repeatedly to look at my phone. And then the reply comes, along with a picture of the admittedly quite diminutive chairs. 'Like toilets with arms,' he says. Oh crap. (No pun intended.)

While I arrange a swap (the furniture site reassures me that 'If your living situation or tastes change, we'll be there to pick up the items you don't want and deliver new ones that work for you'), I explore another kind of homeware sharing. When I spoke to Lennox Cato of *Antiques Roadshow* he informed me that in the early eighteenth century and later, when entertaining, one of the most desirable table decorations was a pineapple. But they were so expensive that people hired them, and in that sense shared them with other fashionable households nearby. As soon as the guests left the dinner table, the pineapple was gathered up and handed to someone waiting outside who would hot-foot to the next venue. It made me consider that sharing 'interior design' wasn't just about furniture – when you think about it, that's not the only thing that IKEA has made 'fast'. It's all the other stuff too, that we don't use very often, and takes up space, like special occasion tableware, or Christmas decorations. And these are things that are also often bought cheaply and then thrown away.

I find a different platform that specialises more in this type of thing, which people can enjoy not just for themselves, but for other occasions when you might need a stylish interior, but don't necessarily want to buy new items: like home staging, film sets, pop-up shops, or for styling interiors for editorial or social media content. This time I decide to list not rent, and recruit Phoebe to help me work out if there is anything remotely desirable in our cupboards between the ageing food processor or ramshackle slow cooker. Then I remember – my sister often gives me lovely vintage things as presents for my birthday and I have a set of 1970s dessert dishes in a kind of smoky red, plus a pair of retro melamine serving spoons. All is not lost. Phoebe styles them artfully and photographs them, then I upload, choosing the suggested fairly low-level rental cost as I figure they're not doing much at the back of the cupboard anyway. Then I wait to see what happens.

According to Josh Nickell of the American Rental Association, furniture rental – beyond having furniture included in your rented home by your landlord (the furnished lets we talked about earlier) – pre-dates the internet by several decades.

'Post-war, the popularity of 'hire purchase' or 'rent to own' was growing in the US, following the lead of the UK brand Radio Rentals which was founded in the 1930s to help people access wireless radios which were still prohibitively expensive. One of the other early innovators was CORT, established in the early 1970s and offering rental 'packages' to those who needed furniture for shorter periods of time. This was at odds with the norm, which was (if you didn't live in a furnished rental property) to have good-quality furniture that had probably been passed to you by your parents or grandparents. Fast furniture was in its infancy and the appeal of rental at this point was less to do with sustainability and more about affordability and convenience: the 'packages' were aimed at those who were maybe new to an area and taking a short-term lease, those in the military, students, newlyweds or perhaps divorcees.

CORT's packages came in a variety of prices and styles. In 1977, their cheapest package was for a studio apartment and cost $20 a month. For $35 a month you could rent enough furniture for a one-bedroom apartment: a bedroom set (dresser, single or double bed, mirror, nightstand and lamp), a dining room set (table and four chairs) and furniture for a living room (couch, coffee table, chair, two end tables and two lamps). There were additional charges too, such as tax, insurance fee, a deposit and delivery – but after a year you had the option of buying everything at a reduced price.'

———

A windy Friday comes when Phoebe can't make it to walk Marley with me, having one of those social engagements that eleven-year-olds do, like trampolining or 'going back to Lola's after school for hot chocolate'. I walk to Marjorie's on my own and Marley rushes out to greet me, throwing himself on his back on the carpeted area outside Marjorie's front door, hoping for some kind of belly tickle from me, which I have never delivered. One day, maybe.

As we are blown together down to the Meadows, I ponder on Marley's dog sharing life, and wonder what he thinks of it, or indeed other dogs who are 'shared' think of it. Are the advantages very much for the humans in the sharing equation, or can dogs benefit too? Yes, dog sharing allows you to have a dog, or just walk a dog in our case, without the commitment and cost. And for the owners, it allows them to have free dog walking and dog care when they need it, or if they are elderly like Marjorie and don't want to go out for walks three times a day.

But for the dogs, who are pack animals, and generally like routine, what does it mean? I ask Shannon Cutts, an author and animal intuitive from Animal Love Languages who has appeared on The Dodo Facebook page herself. 'The big difference between dog sharing and other sharing economy activities is that what is being shared is a conscious, living being. So it's vital to ask, is being 'shared' as positive for a dog as it is for both the sharer and the dog's owner? Generally, dog sharing can keep a dog with their family (and out of a dog shelter) in a productive way that also provides benefits for the 'sharer'. And not only that, it can give a dog a trusted temporary home if the primary guardian or pet parent needs to go away, which often comes with more stability than using kennels. However, some dogs are more sensitive to change, so for dogs who are very young, elderly or recovering from physical or emotional health issues it might be too disruptive. That being said, if a dog suffers from separation anxiety, according to veterinarians and canine behaviourists, sharing may help that dog gain deeper socialisation skills through the opportunity of bonding with other caring humans. So in these types of cases, the benefits can potentially outweigh the downsides.'

Another note about dog sharing: it's not the quickest of processes, and – like me – you might not get the dog you had your heart set on in the first place. Which turned out pretty well in the end in our case: but if you have your heart set on, say, a Hungarian Wirehaired Vizsla, you've got to come to terms with the fact that it's a shallow dog dating pool, and heartbreakers like Aspen are hot property. I'm going to stop using the dating analogy for dogs as it's getting a bit weird now. But you get the picture. You may have to take your time, and make compromises, but that's not necessarily going to be a bad thing in the end.

On that particular Friday, Marley is not convinced by my chosen route, needing some coaxing and a couple of treats (from a little snack bag shaped like a mason jar that Marjorie gives me, along with his ball, every time I collect him). I think this is either because it's windy or because there is not enough entertainment by way of things to sniff on Middle Meadow Walk, although there are plenty of other dogs. This makes me slightly nervous as he can be quite, shall we say, standoffish with them, but certainly not wild, and he never barks, just sort of grumbles at them and pulls on the lead. Today, he potters quite happily along next to me, and I watch other people on the Meadows walking their dogs, and wonder if I seem like one of them, and if I could pass for a Dog Person. Without Phoebe there, I feel slightly awkward with Marley, but he doesn't seem to mind the silence. I try to break it anyway, asking him about his week, and what he's been up to. He sniffs some dubious looking stain on the path. 'Dog stuff, I guess,' I say out loud. A woman walking past looks at me. Maybe people don't make small talk to their dogs. Maybe if I stop doing this, rather than start, I will have more chance of passing for a Dog Person.

I'm not sure if it's because Phoebe isn't here but I suddenly feel very responsible for this little life at the end of the lead. What if something happens to him, what if he eats a poisonous plant, or cuts himself on glass, or runs away and gets hit by a car or . . . It is similar to the feeling you get when you first take your newborn baby out. I sense a rising panic in my chest and shorten the lead to pull Marley closer to me, reaching down to stroke his head. He looks up at me with a questioning expression. 'It's OK,' I say. He stops for a second, as though he's making sure I mean it, then goes back to his little Jack Russell trot, sniffing stains on the path. I smile. He's pretty good company, is Marley.

———

Someone called Kristin (thirties, baby in a buggy with shopping bags hanging from the handles, a bit stressed) borrows my electrical hairstyling brush, just for a day. I hope she doesn't get head lice. My dessert dishes and melamine spoons haven't had any rental requests, though, but I'm guessing like dog sharing this might be a long game. On the same site, I'm quite tempted, as one would be, by an 'Iconic 1970s Modular Orange Melamine Dinner Set for Six People' – especially as I have Julie, Carol and Annie coming round for a pre-Christmas meal next week, and I never have any matching dinner plates. Someone always gets the scratched, ancient Pyrex glass one that's much smaller than all the others, or if they're really unlucky, the Peppa Pig one with Easi-Grip handles. I really should get rid of that now that my children are both in their second decade. But the thing is, although it will only cost £4 to rent the dinner set for a day, because the owner is in London, there's the whole postage thing to consider. I wish that, like the food sharing app, more people were doing this, and somebody like Kim round the corner owned the 'iconic' plates. I'd pop round and get them before you could say *'Abigail's Party'*.

Talking of Christmas – this month, I also rent some wrapping paper. I'm not kidding: Christmas lends itself well to the sharing economy as a lot of the things we use at that time of year, we *only* use at that time of year. And we're all more likely to have extra guests staying too, which means furniture or homeware renting could be a really good way of making sure everyone is catered for, and nobody gets the Peppa Pig plate. I try to hire a Christmas tree as well but this isn't available near us yet – hopefully next year. If you like to 'go large' with your decorations, you can also use stuff sharing platforms to find giant fairy lights, reindeer for your front garden – or how about a projector that gives the effect of huge red and green laughing Santa faces all over the front of your house. Anyone? Incidentally, the wrapping paper arrives in early December, and it's . . . nice. A bit odd. The material it's made of reminds me of those shopping bags that fold up very small and fit in your handbag. But it starts conversations, saves on all that paper waste (not all gift wrap is recyclable, especially if it has metallic details or sticky tape on it) – and it's faff free, as it ties with buttons and string, so no scissors needed.

Back to 'home décor' items. Like many sharing economy things, there is the worry – especially if something is vintage or even antique – that the item will get damaged. Platforms and apps will generally have a deposit or insurance option to protect the owner, but the downside is that this only goes so far. I did suggest I list one of the taxidermy 'specimens' we have (and by 'we' I mean 'he'), as I thought they might get snapped up for perhaps a film or TV set, but he, aka my husband, didn't want to risk it. I can understand that: the puffer fish is surprisingly delicate, a 'one-off' and, in my personal opinion, quite revolting. But you don't marry someone for their taste in stuffed sea creatures.

What else? (And I'm doing the bad news first here, I'm not being negative). As for fashion rental, with furniture and interiors sharing there isn't the same range as you would see from retailers. As well as this, not being able to see items before you choose them to rent can be an issue – the toilet chairs were a pretty good example of that. And while renting furniture is obviously initially less expensive than buying, the monthly expenditure can add up, and there can be 'hidden' costs like delivery and insurance. So a solution to avoiding the negative aspects of fast furniture could be mixing good-quality, built-to-last furniture and homeware pieces with rented items, which you can chop and change depending on trends or what suits your current room layout – or you could just rent things for an occasion, like the coveted iconic dinner set.

Which leads me neatly to the benefits, the main one being of course that you can enjoy gorgeous, unusual furniture and homeware for a lot less cash than buying it – and without the commitment. And in many cases, if you do decide you love what you rented and want to commit, purchasing the thing you've been renting (if you are able to) will be cheaper. It's all very easy too: delivery is usually a lot quicker than retail sites, and collection if you want to swap, or you change your mind, is equally slick. And the big, big benefit at the end of it all is the one that most sharing economy platforms allow us to enjoy: it's a more sustainable choice. The furniture you rent will be refurbished, deep cleaned and then rented out to someone else: the rental platform wants to maximise its lifespan, after all. This allows the furniture to continue its use longer than purchased furniture, reducing environmental impact. And if you're renting from another person, you're using their stuff, and not buying new, so one less thing has been made at a cost to the planet.

The following week, the toilets with arms are collected, thankfully not by the man I shouted at about that cat, and two new – adult size – armchairs arrive. My husband admits they are comfortable and not like toilets in any way, indeed he is spotted a few days later reclining on one of them, feet on the ottoman, *World War II in Colour* on the TV. Jake has started calling the living room the 'Ottoman Empire' and Phoebe declares the whole rented furniture thing to be 'quite the adventure', although I think she's learning sarcasm, so I'm not sure how to take this. In general, it's worked out pretty well, although the Agra table is perhaps not a keeper. But that's the beauty of this: none of it is.

A guide to sharing – part one

FOOD SHARING

What are the benefits?

- Food sharing helps fight waste by preventing unsold or leftover food from ending up in landfill.
- By using food sharing apps you could eat for free – or at least very cheaply.
- The apps can help you get to know a local community of food sharers and make friends.
- If you use restaurant apps, you can find new places to eat nearby and support local businesses.

Do...

Act quickly: listed food can get snapped up in minutes.

Get into the habit of doing a fridge sweep for food that's heading for its Use By date.

Try something new: there's nothing to lose if the food is free.

Don't...

List out-of-date food without saying it's past its Best Before date and may not be at its best.

Forget to collect what you said you would: somebody might be waiting for you.

Have expectations if you collect from restaurants – it's often quite literally a mixed bag.

What to use

In the UK	In the US/Canada	In Australia
OLIO	OLIO	OLIO
Too Good To Go	Little Free Pantries	Bring Me Home
Karma	Food Rescue US	Y Waste
	Goodr	

CLOTHES SHARING

What are the benefits?

- You can support the slow fashion movement and borrow rather than buying new, to help the planet.
- It's a much cheaper way to access designer and higher-priced clothing and accessories.
- You can meet communities of like-minded people, virtually and in-person in your area.
- If you rent out your own clothes, you could earn money to help you pay for more rentals – or for anything else you want.

Do...

Plan ahead – availability isn't as good as on retail clothing websites.

Leave reviews as it helps build a trusted community on the platform you're using.

Experiment – you're not buying the items so there's no commitment.

Don't...

Wash the clothes you borrow: most lenders prefer to take care of cleaning themselves.

Send things back late: somebody else might be renting an item straight after you.

Use online shop pictures for your listing – people want to see you wearing it, not a model.

What to use

In the UK		In the US/Canada
Sharing:	My Wardrobe HQ	Sharing:
HURR	Endless Wardrobe	Tulerie
	Girl Meets Dress	
LOANHOOD	Hirestreet	Style Lend
By Rotation	BagButler (bags)	Rotate
	COCOON (bags)	
Nuw	Bundlee	Designerex
The Killer Muse	(children's)	
Dopplle	For The Creators	
	(maternity)	Rental:
	EcoSki (ski wear)	Rent the Runway
Rental:	The Little Loop	Nuuly
Rotaro	(children's)	Armoire

Fashion to Figure	**In Australia**	Rental:
New York &	Sharing:	GlamCorner
Company	The Volte	All the Dresses
Le Tote	Rent a Dress	Style Theory
Vince Unfold	Designerex	Dress Hire AU
Gwynnie Bee		Rntr

DOG SHARING

What are the benefits?

- You can enjoy forming a relationship with a dog without the cost and commitment of owning one.
- It's a great way to try out dog ownership if you're not sure about it.
- Dogs – and other pets – have a big carbon footprint, so by sharing one you are doing your bit for the planet.
- If you are a dog owner, dog sharing can mean your pet has another family to go to rather than having to use kennels.

Do...

Think hard about your profile and what will make you appeal to dog owners.

Request from multiple owners: the dog you want might be being 'shared' already.

Manage your expectations: some dogs are very popular.

Don't...

Assume you will form a bond with the dog immediately – it takes time.

Sign up unless you're ready to commit to regular contact with a dog.

Share your dog if you think he or she is sensitive to change, very young or elderly, or just not right for it.

What to use

In the UK	In the US/Canada	In Australia
BorrowMyDoggy	Pet Sitters	Dogshare
Share Your Pet	International	BorrowMyPooch
Pawshake	Pawshake	Mad Paws
Trusted	Trusted	
Housesitters	Housesitters	

STUFF SHARING

What are the benefits?

- As a renter, you can access occasional use items cheaply from someone nearby, rather than having to buy them or hire them at a higher cost from a business.
- You can get to know people locally and feel like you're part of a like-minded community.
- It's a lot better for the environment to share household items, rather than leaving them unused or even throwing them out.
- As a lender, you can make money from the things you own and create a new, passive income stream.

Do...

Sign up with a few platforms so that you have access to a bigger range of items.

If you're renting out, be prepared to find that some of your items will be more popular than others.

Try to be accommodating as a sharer (or sharee) when it comes to pick-up and drop-off times.

Don't...

Rent out dirty, broken or malfunctioning items.

Forget to include any instruction booklets with the things you are renting out.

Expect to be able to rent out anything you want, any time – these sharing communities are still growing.

What to use

In the UK
Fat Llama
RentMy
pa-rent
Briskby
KitUp
Party Kit Network
Circular Arts
Network (CAN)
Wrag Wrap
(Christmas wrap
rental)

Whirli (toy rental)
Tool Libraries
(localtools.org)
Libraries of Things
HaveNeed

In the US/Canada
Idle
FriendwithA
Bunz
Rentah
Tool Libraries
(localtools.org)

Libraries of Things
HaveNeed

In Australia
Releaseit
Hire Things
StuffHire
FedeRent
ToolMates
Tool Libraries
(localtools.org)
Libraries of Things
HaveNeed

FURNITURE AND INTERIORS SHARING

What are the benefits?

- When you rent or borrow furniture or homeware, you can tap into an interior style temporarily without having to commit.
- Rented furniture is better for the environment as multiple people can use one item.
- If you have furniture or homeware to rent out, you can make some extra cash from what you already own.
- If you need items for a one-off event, or for content creation or film/TV, it's cheaper and you're more likely to find something that's a one-off.

Do...

Mix rented items with second-hand, upcycled or salvaged furniture, otherwise costs add up.

Shop around: like retail sites, rental platforms will each have their own style.

Dig deep in your cupboards: you never know what you have that could be rented out to others.

Don't...

Rent out something that is really precious or not replaceable, like a family heirloom.

Don't worry about the normal wear and tear to be expected when an item is used as intended.

Feel that you have to like everything you rent, that's the beauty of this: you can send it back!

What to use

In the UK	In the US/Canada	In Australia
Sharing:	CORT	Breeze
shelff	Feather	Green Furniture
HARTH	Fernish	Hub
		CORT
Rental:		Living Edge Rental
Homebound		
Zenkki		
Room Service by		
CORT		
Instant Home		
Loop		

Part Two

The big idea

I don't trust automatics

When I left home, my mother gave me her old car. It was a black Ford Fiesta Bonus that we all called Felicity, with white hubcaps and the smallest possible engine size, the next size down being a food processor. I loved this car: it was beautifully 'manual', not a single electronic element in sight, three doors (why would you need more?) and wind-down windows. Every year, I'd spend more and more on repairs until, one year, the garage told me Felicity hadn't just failed her MOT, but was a write-off.

I managed to drive her, possibly illegally, two streets away to the conveniently placed scrap yard, and the poor girl was then weighed – how undignified. I was given £40, not before my husband had taken a photo of me leaning over her bonnet like, and yet wholly unlike, a Formula 1 Grid Girl, wearing as I was a cardigan and some surprisingly practical looking winter boots. Looking back, posing with the 'Dead Car Driving' was rather morbid, but I wanted to remember those white hubcaps, and the time I drove halfway to Manchester from Oxford with the handbrake on and Felicity just muddled through, although she did feel a little stiff when I joined the M40 at Bicester.

The reason Felicity lasted for fifteen years was because, aside from that trip to Manchester, and the drive to Edinburgh when she became mine, she just wasn't driven very often. And not many cars are. In fact, according to a study from 2018, we are likely to use our car for, on average, just nine hours a week – for the remaining 159 hours it sits on the driveway, in the garage, in a car park or outside a place of work. So why does this matter? I found a report from 2020[9] by the IEA (International Energy Agency) which found that transport was responsible for 24 per cent of direct CO_2 emissions, and we all know by now that CO_2 emissions aren't good for much at all.

While on an individual level, many people are trying to fly less and perhaps cut down on using their cars, for journeys when you do need a car, borrowing one, aka car sharing, can make a real difference. That's because every car shared takes ten off the road – and when you consider that even for an electric vehicle, 46% of its total carbon footprint is generated before it has even been driven (what?!) the benefits start to become even clearer.

So how does car sharing work? To most people it might not seem that different from heading to the car hire desk when you land at an airport. The car's not yours, you're only using it for a few days, and you're sharing it with other people, right? Well, rental like this does have a place, in that you can use a car that isn't yours, instead of buying one and

9 https://www.iea.org/topics/transport

having it sit there unused. But car *sharing* is a bit different, in the same way that renting clothes from a company that owns them is different from peer-to-peer sharing, which means renting them from other people like you and me. Car sharing platforms and apps provide car owners with a way to earn money by renting out their own vehicle when they're not using it, and on the other side of the equation, they allow those who don't have a car – or have a need for an extra one – to rent one locally, usually for however long they want. So, multiple people from a certain area can actually have access to one vehicle.

Car sharing works a lot like other types of sharing, although the identity checks are understandably more thorough. But – just like with clothes, dogs, food, stuff and furniture – signing up, creating a profile and then requesting what you want to borrow is pretty much the extent of it. And how it differs from traditional car rental is that you can rent a car on the next street, for the weekend or just an hour: it's up to you – as long as it's available.

For the car owner, this means the chance to make some extra cash. But the other big benefit of peer-to-peer car sharing is that it connects drivers with stationary cars in their neighbourhood. If you're wondering what's wrong with stationary cars, I'll tell you: journeys in towns and cities are longer because drivers need more time to find parking spaces, and having cars driving around in circles looking for one (we've all done it) leads to congestion and an increase in emissions. But if these stationary cars could be used for even just part of the time they were sitting there, it would help make cities more efficient. We'll come back to parking soon, because the sharing economy has a solution for that too.

That's not all – of course it's not, this is the sharing economy, which is never about just one thing. Having a single car used by more than one person doesn't just mean fewer parked cars getting in the way of me finding a space large enough so that I can reverse park in one go (rather than do the Park of Shame when four cars are waiting to get past and you drive in at the wrong angle and know you've ruined it, but instead of just starting again you try to straighten up in a series of micro-movements that inevitably nudge the car in front. Then you mount the kerb just to let the now seven cars pass and drive out and start all over again.) No, it means fewer new cars on the road. If more people start car sharing, fewer people will buy new cars, or second cars. And last but not least, car sharing creates the potential for more people to use electric vehicles. Because although the current high cost of electric cars can make them unappealing as a permanent purchase, they are a lot more enticing when you're just renting them. And once you try one, you never know, you might change your mind.

———

For me, the desire to experiment with car sharing rapidly becomes a necessity when our Vauxhall Zafira Exclusiv (correct spelling) developed a 'quirk'. It's a classic 7-seater 'Mum Bus', which I always think sounds like a cloud formation: Cumulo Mumbus. Anyway, by 'quirk' I mean a kind of juddering jumpy thing that will probably need immediate attention. I did mention it to the garage at its last service, but the (rather dour) Jim told me we'd 'need to wait for the light to come on'. Which light, I don't know. But the judder has indeed got worse, and on the day in question, the fabled light finally comes on. When I look up in the manual to see what this light actually means (hoping the problem's solvable by filling up with something like water or oil), the not-very-well-thumbed book in the glove compartment tells me that said light means 'engine'. That doesn't sound good. Or very specific . . . isn't a car *mainly* an engine? The manual also tells me that when this light comes on I must NOT drive the car and that I must Immediately Take It To A Mechanic.

The timing of this is not great. As a family, we can often go a few days without using the car, meaning that occasionally, nobody can remember where it's parked, and we wander the streets by the Meadows looking for a roof rack, or the distinctive gaffer-taped-on wing mirror which, when it's sunny, catches the light, as though the car is winking. However, this is not a week when we won't use the car, as the next day, I have one of those perfect storms of parenting to get through, while my husband is working in Glasgow. A plate-spinning two hours where an orthodontist appointment for Jake coincides with Bike Club, followed by Guides, to which I have to take another child as well as Phoebe. To say that this was doable without a car, in the depths of winter when it gets dark in Edinburgh at about 3pm, would be a lie. And taxiing the whole affair would probably set me back more than the price of sorting out the judder itself.

So that evening I download a car sharing app. It's a lot more official looking than the sharing economy apps I've used so far, but that's understandable: borrowing someone's car needs a bit more of a 'belt-and-braces' approach than eating someone's unwanted radishes. After registering the usual name/address type details, I go through a series of checks that involve taking pictures of my driving licence, followed by uploading a selfie of me, for facial recognition purposes, or some such thing. Taking the picture is trickier than I imagine and all vanity has to be left at the door. The app keeps telling me to move closer and then move back, as I try to get my head into the required oval shape, and the resulting picture is, and I'm being kind to myself here, not one for the mantelpiece.

Finally I'm approved, as I should be, having had my licence for a long time and pretty much not done anything bad – apart from the time I was pregnant with Phoebe and the sun was in my eyes on Easter Road. I drove the car (a Honda as I recall), very gently I would like to add, into the back of the one in front. But thankfully, my incredibly large belly was enough to make the owner of said car, which now had a broken number plate, not only tell me it didn't matter but hug me, slightly pityingly. I think this was because when she asked nervously if I was 'about to pop' (which always struck me as a strange way of describing giving birth), I told her I was in fact only six months pregnant. 'You're awfy big, hen. What a shame for you,' she said, as she drove off to get her number plate fixed.

Anyway, the end result of this shame, aka Phoebe, is keen to know if she will be able to go to Bike Club and Guides the following night, so I set about searching for a car to 'borrow'. I search by postcode and the app tells me to 'Take a look at some of the highest rated and most popular cars in my area'. I've been fooled by this before, and if you don't know what I mean, one word: Aspen. So do I *really* want the most popular ones, or will they be desirable, but ultimately unattainable?

There's a red Škoda quite nearby which the owner describes as a 'working car' (as opposed to?) and apologises in advance for dog hair on the seats. That'll be why it's only £2 an hour. There's also a more pricey (£4 an hour) Toyota Yaris with a headless person sitting on the bonnet, which I hope is to do with the crop of the photo, and isn't actually included. I also spot a BMW 3 Series M Sport which I immediately place on my mental 'No' pile because of a) all the letters and numbers in the name which suggest it's fast and b) because it's £8 an hour, and if that's what we're doing I might as well get a taxi. I also decide against the Yaris as it's automatic and I don't trust automatics, in the same way that I don't trust microwaves, because I don't understand *how* they work. I suppose this could mean I shouldn't use, for example, a smart phone, or a laptop, but I like these things so for them I'm willing to overlook the gaps in my knowledge.

I land on a Vauxhall Corsa which looks like something that someone who doesn't like driving other people's cars should drive. It's also 1.4 miles away which doesn't sound that far, but then nor did the carpet cleaner. The description says it comes with 'all the other bells and whistles you need to make your trip as comfortable as possible'. I ponder this and decide that neither bells nor whistles will make this trip, which I'm already becoming slightly anxious about, remotely comfortable. I won't even put the radio on, I suspect, needing to concentrate as I will on the fact that reverse gear might be in a different position to where it is on Cumulo Mumbus, or that perhaps the indicators will be on the opposite side of the steering wheel. Or maybe they're always on the same side? I put these thoughts aside long enough to book the Corsa for £12 (four hours at £3 an hour) and this bargain price compared to a taxi is the only thing that helps me to get to sleep that night, instead of worrying about where the windscreen wiper control will be.

Another thought goes round my head as I lie in bed: maybe Cumulo Mumbus can be listed on the app after all, once given the 'all clear' by the garage. If car sharers are openly admitting to dog hairs, then maybe I should just upload it on the app as it is, unvaleted, then say it's a 'working car' and allude to the chances of finding anything from a sock to the remains of a Magic Bag in the side pockets. Or a snail, apparently, which is the answer when I ask the family what the worst thing is they've ever found in the car. I can't say I'm a snail fan (although I could be persuaded if there was quite a lot of garlic and butter involved) but I do quite like the idea of creating a micro ecosystem on the back seat. Surely that's good for the planet too?

———

As with all of my sharing experiments, a delve into the past is in order to find out how long we've been doing some of these things that might seem new, but probably aren't. I get in touch with Alan Pisarski, a US-based writer, analyst and consultant in transportation. From him I find out that almost as soon as cars arrived on the roads in any quantity, at the start of the twentieth century, their owners were on the lookout for a way to cash in on their ownership. This had everything to do with the financial side of sharing and absolutely nothing to do with the environment, of course: car ownership was increasing exponentially and very few people saw that as a bad thing. Enter the 'jitneys', which were private cars that picked up paying passengers for a small fee. In fact 'jitney' is slang for a nickel, or five cents, which was the fee charged when the idea took off in the 1910s in the US and Canada.

One of the first mentions of jitneys in the press was in the *Toronto Daily Star* on 29 January 1915, under the headline 'The Jitneys Are Coming'. The article read: 'A new form of opposition to trolley cars has arisen. It is the Jitney – or the five-cent auto ride . . . No franchise is granted, anybody that can buy one can operate it wherever he can get enough business to make it pay . . . It has been found that an ordinary auto can make money in the business, and everyday sees more and more of them engaging in it.'[10]

So this was more of a precursor to the 'rideshare' or 'ridehailing' model: we're all familiar with these apps – they're in the news often enough. This is a perfect opportunity for us to pause and talk about them, briefly. Because for many, when you hear the phrase 'sharing economy', a certain rideshare app is what springs to mind. I understand why, because when the concept was born, it was based around the 'collaborative consumption' that is also the basis of the sharing economy. In other words, technology allows people to offer services peer-to-peer, as well as goods – so in theory, drivers could make some extra income using their car as a taxi on the side.

A couple of big-name rideshare apps became successful in this area, and also became an example – rightly or wrongly – of the sharing economy, alongside of course Airbnb, which we'll talk about later. This book isn't about stories from Silicon Valley, but suffice to say, it got complicated.

---

10 https://driving.ca/

Low wages, lack of rights and benefits for workers, safety, and the impact on the competition are just a few of the other issues that have arisen for the platforms in this ridesharing space. It's also worth considering if these apps should be thought of as part of the sharing economy at all: surely it's only sharing, and not simply a taxi service, if the driver is going that way anyway. Otherwise, what exactly is the under-used asset being shared?

By 1918, the number of jitneys had fallen considerably, as governments, in the same way that they would with the rideshare platforms a century later, clamped down. But that wasn't the end of the concept: the jitney prevailed in many of the Black neighbourhoods that taxi companies refused to enter, and evolved into 'dollar vans' in New York in the 1980s. These are unofficial minibus shuttle services that operate where subways and other buses don't (or won't), in other words, in low-income neighbourhoods that contain large immigrant communities. A final jitney reference is to a play by August Wilson, called simply *Jitney*, which was written and set in the 1970s. It's about five taxi drivers in Pittsburgh who are fighting against the authorities. The more things change, the more they . . . oh, you know the rest.

————

The following day, the car sharing app reminds me that I'm collecting the Vauxhall Corsa that afternoon. Around 2pm I duly set off to walk the 1.4 miles to collect it, leaving earlier than necessary to take a slight detour via Kim's, where I pick up some free almond croissants for the kids – then worry that they will get flaky pastry on the car seats. My walking route takes me out of my usual area of Edinburgh and into an unfamiliar network of streets near the Union Canal – this, for those of us who don't know, which included me until I looked it up, runs from Falkirk to Edinburgh, and was built to bring coal to the capital. That has nothing to do with this particular expedition, however, other than to note that 1.4 miles takes a bit longer to walk than I thought. Eventually, however, I find the address in question, in a large development of modern flats, where each section has an area of its own private parking and garden, with marked numbered bays corresponding with the flat numbers. And there is my Vauxhall Corsa in its glory, awaiting my heavy-handed (-footed) clutch control with eager anticipation.

I am using a fancy bit of tech on the car sharing app that allows me to unlock the car with my phone. I love a bit of tech, however this feels a bit more serious than asking to walk someone's Shar Pei. But the app takes me through it patiently, first requesting another selfie which again is so unflattering I briefly wonder if there is a sharing economy for Botox. Then, I have to take 'condition' photos of all four sides of the car. I speculate if any of the neighbours are looking out of their windows at me, trying to work out what an anxious-looking woman is doing in their car park stroking her forehead lines and taking pics of a Vauxhall Corsa. Photos taken, the app then allows me to unlock the door (by tapping a button: witchcraft). Once in the car, I have to take yet more photos of the interior and then, with immense trepidation, I start the engine using a button, silently longing for the simpler times of Felicity with her giant key and choke.

The car starts and immediately I rev it far too much. If the onlooking neighbours didn't see me take the selfie, they will now definitely be peering through their blinds, and just to make sure, I produce a horrible clutch grinding noise as I put the poor vehicle in reverse. This is going well. The car feels very low down and sporty compared to Cumulo Mumbus and the accelerator and clutch are much more sensitive. I'm quite grateful for the large car park as it gives me a chance to take a couple of moments to get used to the car before I get out onto the main road – but I have to get to school to collect Phoebe so I don't have time for a full driving lesson. Minutes later, I'm on busy Slateford Road, revving like Lewis Hamilton, with the windscreen wipers wiping non-existent rain away at top speed. I'm terrified, but all I can think of is the fact that I might be leaving sweaty bum-cheek marks on the seat. Nobody is going to give me five stars for that.

By the time I get to school, my heart rate has dropped considerably, the headlights are off (it is broad daylight after all) and the windscreen wipers have stopped their frantic wiping. Phoebe is most excited to see me parked in a different car, or any car at all, as we usually walk home. 'It smells like an Uber' she declares and starts pressing every available button on the dashboard, resulting in the windscreen wipers starting up again, incredibly, even faster than before. She wants to put Heart FM on the radio but I bark 'NO!' at her as we drive off to Bike Club, needing as I do to fully concentrate on stopping the windscreen wipers. Maybe the 'bells and whistles' wouldn't have been so bad after all.

And so the perfect storm of parenting begins and Phoebe is delivered to Bike Club, Jake is taken to the orthodontist, Phoebe is collected, Jake is collected, Phoebe's friend is collected, Phoebe is taken to Guides (etc., etc.), and I become more and more confident with the perky little Corsa. Power steering makes my usual eleven-point turns merely five-point, and by the time I collect Phoebe from Guides I let her put Heart FM on and we sing along to Bruno Mars all the way home. 'I'll miss this car,' she says mournfully as I drop her home for the last time before I head off to return it. 'We'll see it again one day,' I reassure her.

It's dark as I head back along Slateford Road, shouting Dua Lipa's 'New Rules' at the top of my voice. 'One: don't pick up the phone.' I bellow, turning into the side street where the Vauxhall Corsa lives, but I don't get to rule number two, because at this point I realise each section of the flats, and the corresponding car parks, look very similar. And also, concerningly, quite unfamiliar in the dark. I pull in and double-check the address, which suddenly doesn't seem to correspond with where I remember the car being when I collected it. Or is it just because other cars have now parked there too? Or is it because I am directionally challenged? Whichever it is, it doesn't take me long to realise that I can't find the place to which I'm supposed to return the car. As my app counts down and reminds me it's time to take the car back (YES I KNOW), my phone decides to simultaneously warn me that I've got a low battery. Dua Lipa's new rules aren't going to help me now.

A few circuits of the interlinked car parks later and I now have four minutes to return the car. I take a gamble on a space that *feels* like the one I picked up the car from. I think I remember that section of box hedge. And there was definitely a silver car next to it. But is that one silver? It's hard to tell in the dark – maybe it's white. A man exits the flats and looks at me. I try to read his expression: is it 'You don't need Botox, daylight doesn't flatter anyone at this time of year', or perhaps it's 'That's the right space love, well done'. It's probably more likely to be 'Why are you sitting outside my flat in a Vauxhall Corsa looking like you want to cry?'. Anyway, the deed is done, the car is parked, and all I have to do now, after hastily brushing almond croissant crumbs off the seats, is take many, many photos with a phone that's now on 8 per cent, and get a taxi home. I briefly consider phoning my husband, who is now back from Glasgow, to ask him to come and pick me up, and then I remember the WHOLE REASON FOR DOING THIS IN THE FIRST PLACE.

———

Before apps – like the one I'm using – made it easy to borrow a car from your neighbour, were there any pre-internet attempts at this peer-to-peer car sharing, I wonder? This is a bit different from the jitneys, as it's about letting someone else actually borrow the car, not just get a lift, while you do the driving. I ask Susan Shaheen, a UC Berkeley professor and sustainable transportation research director. From her, I find out about one of the earliest peer-to-peer car sharing experiments, which took place in Europe just after the Second World War. The project was a cooperative that was started in Zurich, known as *Selbstfahrergemeinschaft*: I used the power of Google to translate this, roughly, as 'Car renter community'. Unsurprisingly, the focus of the scheme was about sharing resources for financial reasons, rather than environmental, as in 1948 not everyone could afford to buy a car, and the priority was getting access to one, not reducing the number of vehicles on the roads.

Susan also tells me about other attempts at car sharing initiatives in the 1970s, for example one called *Procotip* that was started in Montpellier, France, and another called *Witkar* in Amsterdam. Despite their benefits, these efforts were not sustainable. It wasn't then until towards the end of the century – or millennium, to be more precise – that the concept began gathering strength again, just in time for more advanced technologies to make it easier to implement and scale, and bring it into mainstream use.

All the while, in the background, one type of vehicle sharing – and probably the least structured and regulated – continued. I refer of course to the (now practically lost) art of hitchhiking. It's such a familiar concept it took me a while to even think of it as a precursor of the sharing economy, taking on as it did a name – and life – of its own. But it's probably one of the most popular types of car sharing there is, and as old as, well, I'm about to find out. I go back to Alan Pisarski to ask him about hitchhiking and how it fell from grace.

'From the first part of the twentieth century onwards, the sight of someone holding a thumb out to get a lift was incredibly normal.' He's right – I remember it myself when growing up. 'I always use the example of my daughter,' he continues.

'She's grown up now, with her own children, but when she was younger she would hitchhike everywhere. More than I knew about at the time, certainly – to work, to college . . . it was just part of life. Now she has kids of her own and she wouldn't dream of letting them do that. But the shift wasn't about hitchhiking itself – it was society. I think we've become more over-protective and teach our children not to interact with strangers. And although some governments used scare tactics in their campaigns to get people to stop hitching rides, and screenwriters used (and still use) hitchhiking as a plot device in horror films – it's actually not as dangerous statistically as it was made out.

'There are other factors at play here: more people own cars, that's a big shift. And of course if you own a car, you're unlikely to need a lift. That's why in developing countries hitchhiking has survived as an early form of ridesharing. But in the developed world, we're more likely to own a car. With that comes big, fast roads – freeways or motorways – which are another factor, because pedestrians are generally banned from these cross-country routes, so hitchhiking long distance has become harder. Some US states even prohibit it now.'

So it seems what hitchhiking *did* do was create a true sharing economy model in that as a hitchhiker, you are using the under-used asset, which in this case is a seat in a car. And the driver is going that way anyway, so you're not being taken specifically to your destination, unlike the jitneys or indeed many of the rideshare apps that we use today. Unless of course we actually select a 'car pool' or sharing option on these apps, or pick one that specialises in cutting down on the number of cars used per commute. Sometimes the precursors of sharing economy apps do it better than the apps themselves.

―――――

Cars aren't the only kind of transport you can share. You will probably have seen, especially if you live in a big city, bike and scooter sharing programs that have popped up in many places over the last decade. These tend to be funded by local councils, and are often sponsored: in Edinburgh, until recently, there was a bike share scheme that sadly seems to have suffered, like many things, at the hands of the pandemic. There are also big companies who work with cities to offer both bikes and scooters for people to rent: these programs are aimed at encouraging bike use by individuals who might not otherwise use a bicycle. They have their opponents, though, with some people believing that they attract inexperienced and unskilled riders, many less likely to wear helmets, making them a danger on the roads.

Although these types of schemes are often considered part of the sharing economy, it strikes me that they aren't that different from the airport car hire model mentioned before. A company owns a load of bikes and/or scooters – you pay to hire one. But what about 'real' bike sharing: and by that I mean, borrowing someone else's bike when they're not using it? That's a thing too, although only a few peer-to-peer bike sharing platforms have really got off the ground. Which is a shame, because there are plenty of benefits to doing it, similar of course to the benefits of car sharing: why own a new, expensive thing if you're only going to use it occasionally? The added benefit with bike sharing of course is that it allows people to travel without using fuel and producing emissions and can help create a culture of eco-friendly transportation. The more cyclists there are on the road, the more drivers – and infrastructure – must adapt. And as a further consequence, air quality will improve into the bargain. As well as this, cycling itself comes with fitness benefits – and renting a bike from someone else could mean you get to try cycling before committing to buying a bike of your own, similar to trying a PlayStation VR headset, but hopefully more successful.

In our household, we have three bikes, all ridden with varying degrees of frequency and enthusiasm. None of them are mine. That's not to say I can't ride a bike, which you might expect, having read about my driving skills. But *au contraire*: growing up as I did in the bike-friendly city of Oxford, I was a keen cyclist until I moved up to Scotland and took possession of the aforementioned Felicity the Fiesta. And so it is now that I have somehow not sat on a bike for about twenty years (probably more) and I am under pressure from my family to put the old 'it's just like riding a bike' adage to the test. Or is it? The main excerptor of this pressure is my husband, having as he does a much more 'outdoorsy' demeanour than me and often lamenting that we're not 'like normal families' who attach five bikes to the back of their Cumulo Mumbus and head off up a Munro or whatever normal families do. Munros are Scottish mountains higher than 3,000 feet, and there are 282 of them. Outdoorsy people play a game where they climb and therefore 'bag' them; my current Munro score is 0 and will probably remain that way.

My husband has a very expensive bike and lots of accessories to go with it, like special shorts with padding – which the children gleefully call his 'nappies' – and panniers, and other things that I don't understand, or care to. We've talked about buying me a bike, so I am forced to just use it, but that's where this could go very wrong. And because we are decidedly not buying things at the moment – and of course borrowing, renting or swapping instead – what a perfect solution the sharing economy could be. I can borrow someone's bike, and if I like cycling as much as I did in Oxford a long time ago, then we might even stand a chance of actually becoming a 'normal' family.

My husband has welcomed this sharing economy activity considerably more enthusiastically than any others so far, apart from perhaps that Magic Bag that came with quiches in it, or the time Marley sat on his foot. I am buoyed by his enthusiasm, that is until I discover that what he has in store is not a mere circuit of the Meadows. 'We can cycle up Arthur's Seat!' he announces. I'm not certain how far, or how steep, that is, but I'm pretty sure that it's not the same as cycling from Botley into Oxford, which back in my heyday took me about twenty minutes, with not a bus lane nor a helmet in sight. That was the 1980s for you. I was probably also drunk/smoking/eating a Findus Crispy Pancake, or something else that sounds reckless and not like the kind of thing we would ever do these days.

There are only a few options for renting a bike from someone in Edinburgh – probably not as many as in other cities, but that will hopefully change soon. One option is to use a specific bike-sharing platform, and there are a couple of these (remember I list the names of different companies in the sections at the end of Part 1 and Part 2 of the book). You can also usually find bikes on stuff sharing platforms, which is what I go for. But it seems the difficult part is just beginning, because once I have selected the category 'Bikes' and zoomed in on a map of Edinburgh, my knowledge – or lack of it – when it comes to bikes – is thrown into sharp relief. It all seems to have got quite complicated since Oxford in the 1980s, when you just bought any old bike from a second-hand bike shop as long as it had a chain on, and then painted it (rainbow colours in my case) and put on a basket. Men's bikes had crossbars, women's didn't. And that was about it, as I recall. Now it's all 'Hybrids',

'Track Bikes' and 'Cruisers'. I feel a bit out of my depth to say the least.

I hastily scroll past a listing titled 'Ladie's Hybrid Bike!' (sic) due to punctuation concerns, skip over 'CITY BIKE ELOPS 900 STEP-THROUGH - DARK GREEN' due to too much information and pass on simply 'Bike' due to lack of it. Then I spot it – a silver 'Ridgeback Vanteo' which is apparently both 'comfortable' and 'the perfect bike to meander through the city streets on'. I like the sound of 'meandering'. I don't remember doing that recently, if ever. It's being rented out by someone called Caroline who also rents out a 'Child's Red Bike' and lives, crucially, this side of Nutbush. I submit a request to borrow Caroline's 'Ridgeback', then google 'Can you forget how to ride a bike?'.

There will be no miracles here

I used to work in an advertising agency as a writer. The agency occupied the second and third floors of an ugly office block in the New Town of Edinburgh, which is mainly elegant Georgian houses, making the ugly office block look even uglier. On the second floor of the building were the Suits: the account managers who dealt with clients, as well as the finance department and the bosses. On the third floor were the rest of us: the Creatives (my department), the studio, production, and a few tiny meeting rooms with classic 90s décor like bright orange walls, and beanbags and lava lamps. And as much as we wanted to think it looked just like the Saatchi offices, with a dartboard and a foosball table (*Friends* was very much the TV show of the moment), the truth is that it was still an ugly, airless, modern office with fluorescent lighting and a carpet that looked like it harboured skin cells from the first time lava lamps were de rigueur.

The Suits would arrive early, as they worked a lot harder than us Creatives, who would saunter out of the lifts at about

9.20, usually hungover, sometimes still drunk. We didn't know about *Mad Men* but we were doing our damnedest to perpetuate the myth that the best ideas came when you were either half-cut or recovering from being half-cut. The reality was pretty much the opposite. When we weren't 'brainstorming' in the pub, ignoring calls on our flip phones from the Suits, we were often found lying on the aforementioned beanbags, ordering bacon-and-egg rolls from the café downstairs, or throwing up said rolls in the tiny, also airless, bathrooms situated by the lifts on each floor. Which doesn't paint a pretty picture, and I hasten to add that I loved this job, and made friends for life there, some of whom are mentioned elsewhere in this book. But what I am talking about here is productivity. We *had* to go to the office in the morning, unless we were genuinely ill (drinking Slippery Nipples at 3am in Fingers, a bar which doesn't need any further description, didn't count), or we'd had some kind of family emergency, which would be checked up on, and had better be serious.

This was how work – or workspaces – erm . . . worked. You had an office and whether you were productive or not, you commuted to a heated building that was lit up like the proverbial Blackpool Illuminations. And this was the way. Until . . . lockdown. Most of us suddenly had to start working from home, which came, as we know, with a whole set of pros and cons of its own. Lack of in-person human interactions and children interrupting Zoom calls because they needed their bums wiped made some of us miss the office . . . while getting to lie in bed until 8.58am and work in your pyjama bottoms made some of us wish we didn't have to go back there ever again.

Working from home suits some people and some types of job, and doesn't suit others. But working in an office all day every day doesn't make sense on many levels. It doesn't always make people productive, as I and my fellow creative department members proved in the 1990s. And it's not great for the environment to run big offices. But is it necessarily better to work from home? That's been debated, and the answer is: not particularly. When your home becomes your office, your commute might fall out of the carbon equation, but you have to take into account what's going on in your home, which might actually be less energy efficient. This is where hybrid working comes in: a combination of home and office working which can reduce the environmental costs of running a big office, as well as improve productivity and help employees have a better work–life balance. But what if you don't want to sit at your kitchen table, or don't have the space to work from home?

Here's one idea: space sharing. Space is an 'asset' just like stuff is, it's just a lack of stuff. But it can still be under-used, and therefore be shared, and this can provide a whole load of benefits for both the sharer and the sharee. Co-working spaces are one type of workspace sharing: usually in the form of an office space that is used by many companies of different sizes, and offering a place for workers to use if they need or want to, in combination with working at home or elsewhere. For smaller companies this means you only pay (often month by month) for the space you are actually going to use, without any locked-in contracts. And these days the spaces are often designed to reduce carbon emissions by sharing utilities, appliances and supplies.

Another type of workspace sharing allows you to book tables in cafés, restaurants or hotels, by the hour on an app.

Using these spaces means remote workers can make use of electricity, heating and Wi-Fi that is switched on anyway, rather than using what may be less efficient in their own home. Getting out of the house has also been proven to be better for mental health; during the lockdowns, many people reported increased work stress, an inability to switch off and a feeling of disconnect from their colleagues. So is this hybrid way of working a better solution? Fewer big ugly offices, more use of space that's sitting unused, and a bit of homeworking thrown into the mix, but only if it doesn't drive you crazy? Of course, not everyone can pick and choose. Many jobs mean you have to be at a certain place at a certain time. But for the rest of us, if there's a better way, isn't it worth a try?

For me, experimenting with workspace sharing becomes a necessity when the office space that I've been renting on and off for a while is needed back by the owners. As well as that, in our new home, work space – like storage space – is not exactly at a premium, and as much as I sometimes like to sit and work at the kitchen table, it can all feel a bit too 2020 for my liking. So I sign up with a sharing app that connects people who need somewhere to work with spaces, such as restaurants, cafés and hotels. This helps the 'hosts' – ie the hospitality venues in question – reach new potential customers, look busy during quiet times, and make money from food and drink – although there's generally no pressure to buy.

Some sharing apps also include spaces in other people's offices, while others allow people to rent out space in their own homes for people to work or have meetings in, or even, if you are a musician, rehearse in. You can also rent out your home as a photography or film set, but personally I don't think there's much call among the movie making community for a 'messy Edinburgh home with questionable table in the hall, uninvited cat and a teenager's room that smells like Chinese food'. Might be worth a shot, though as it could work for something arthouse. In all these cases, what the sharing economy does is allow us to make use of what is already there, access more choice, save a bit of money . . . and even help the environment a bit too.

———

After a few weeks of working at home, I am more than ready to try out the workspace sharing app. I'm tired of not only how scruffy I always look (if I can make that hair wash last four days with some Dutch braiding, who cares if it's started to smell like the hutch of my late guinea pig?), but also how dull I have become. Having no other human interactions aside from on Zoom calls, and no other 'experiences' other than the school run, doesn't make my conversation that scintillating. 'There's leftover risotto in the fridge for lunch if you want it.' 'Have you put the dishwasher on?' 'Have you got anything to go in a dark wash?' I always say the last one pointedly as my husband never separates colours. So I decide that booking a workspace in a trendy hotel or bar nearby, washing my hair and donning an actual outfit (rented of course) will result in me having an exciting day, during which I will meet interesting people, and then return home full of hilarious anecdotes that don't relate in any way to the white goods in our kitchen.

Booking on the workspace sharing app is easy, with a map showing me a variety of nearby places where I can find a table or desk: a mix of bars, hotels and cafés. Some are even (very nice) restaurants that only serve food in the evening, presumably allowing the business to generate extra cash during the day, or just make use of their space. When you tap on your chosen venue, the app brings up all the important information, about things like Wi-Fi, parking, whether seats have power points near them, the sort of thing that you might not necessarily think of until you get there. After some deliberation, I choose a nearby hotel, and book my time slot – to do this you also have to choose what your 'booking purpose' is from 'A space to work', 'A meeting room' or 'Something else', although I'm not entirely sure what 'Something else' would be as this is a workspace sharing app.

The following day I get dressed in my current favourite clothes rental, a brown cord blazer by a brand called Soeur, which, when I research it, is apparently all about 'androgynous allure'. It's also all about pretty eye-watering prices which is why I'm glad said blazer is rented. Pleased with my joggers-free attire and clean hair and looking forward to a lack of kitchen-related repartee, I head off to the hotel as soon as the children have been dispatched to school, which seems adventurous in itself, after what feels like centuries of working from home.

The hotel is very mid-century modern, all uncomfortable-looking wooden chairs and patterned wallpaper, and it reminds me of a kind of newer, brighter version of the room my mother would have watched the coronation in. A woman greets me warmly at the reception desk, and before I've even had a chance to mention the workspace app or tell her my name and reservation details, she directs me to a room several floors up in the lift. When I get there, I am cheered to find not only a breathtaking view of the castle (which has snow on its battlements today) and what appears to be free refreshments, but enough – and not too many – interesting-looking people. They are a mix of ages, all at laptops and gathered in groups around a huge table (also mid-century). I didn't quite anticipate the shared table but it's very big, and there aren't *that* many other people there, so I choose a seat and settle down to get on with my work.

I am enjoying a change of scene, although I am somewhat unused to being socially acceptable and not doing things like muttering 'fcksaaake' when I type four sentences in capitals without noticing, or peering at the screen as though it's one of those Magic Eye drawings, because I'm resisting getting reading glasses. I help myself to coffee, and a glass of water (not fizzy, due to anxieties about public burping) and spot that there are also some breakfast-type things on a table at the side of the room: fruit, pastries, bagels – even some porridge. When in Rome, I think to myself, and fill a plate up with strawberries and those little coiled French pastries with egg custard and raisins.

As the morning progresses, I am thoroughly enjoying the experience, and look forward to telling my husband about this sharing economy triumph later. As I smile smugly to myself and nail Wordle in three, the woman in the group next to me at the table leans over and asks me 'How are you getting on?' She's so cool that she's wearing what looks like a ski hat, even though the room is quite warm. I wonder for a second if she's talking about my pastry, Wordle or the space-sharing experience in general. But as they are all brilliant, I decide it doesn't matter, so, once I've swallowed a particularly stubborn raisin, I reply 'Tremendous', and then realise I don't think I've ever used that word before. It just *feels* like the right thing to do in that moment, like wearing the ski hat maybe does for her.

The coffee and sugar has made me incredibly productive and it's already noon. I'm considering popping out for a breath of fresh air and maybe a sandwich, although I'm pretty full from the pastries. But before I can even close my laptop, a man across the table stands up and appears to be about to make an announcement. 'Everyone . . . everyone . . .' he says, looking round the table, which has filled up during the morning. I hadn't noticed this, being engrossed in my work as I have been. And Wordle, which was a tough one today (Egret, since you ask). 'I'd like to get everyone's ideas,' he continues, pulling a white board across the patterned carpet and positioning it at the end of the table. On what, I wonder. What to have for lunch? Whether Wordle is becoming harder? The mid-century aesthetic? This is certainly more collaborative than I had envisaged but I suppose we are sharing, so maybe sharing *ideas* is part of that. I must have looked keener than I felt in that moment because the man, who is in his forties and wearing enormous, Eric Morecambe-esque glasses that just about balance out his equally enormous beard, looks straight at me.

I delay speaking by leaning back in my chair and rolling up my sleeves, but such actions can only buy one so much time, and then I am forced to reply. The people round the table, who I now note to be about twenty in number, look expectantly at me and I wonder if it is possible to say something so generic that it answers any question, even one like this that you don't understand in the slightest. Eric Morecambe is poised by the white board clutching a large marker pen, and Ski Hat has tipped her head to one side as if she is now wondering how tremendously it really is going for me.

I glance at the sleeve I've just rolled up and then I remember the description of the brand who made my blazer. 'Androgynous allure,' I mutter, and as Eric Morecambe writes these two words quite slowly onto the white board, I use the ten seconds he takes to do so as a distraction, grab my laptop and bag, and stumble out the door into the corridor. I don't wait to see how my 'idea' has gone down, and indeed find out what the idea was for, or what sort of meeting I had unwittingly become a part of. No wonder there had been so much free food: the porridge should have aroused my suspicions. I leave, smiling wanly at the receptionist who initiated the farce, and vow never to return to this hotel. Although, with an anecdote to return home with, a morning's work done and Wordle cracked in three, I will definitely be using the workspace sharing app again.

———

The following Saturday I am due to pick up Caroline's Ridgeback bike at noon, which we've arranged via the messaging function on the platform. I've rented it from her for two days, which is the minimum, at £12 a day – the maximum rental is three weeks which seems like a long time. Maybe she doesn't like it that much. Anyway, she lives in Prestonfield, which is walkable but I decide to take Cumulo Mumbus, put the seats down in the back and drive the bike home. This is because I'm not that sure about having my maiden voyage on the Ridgeback a) on my own and b) between Prestonfield and our home, a lot of which is uphill. Well maybe 'uphill' is a bit strong: more 'at a slight gradient'. But I would rather remember how to ride a bike (if indeed I am able to) on a flat surface, and with supervision/moral support from my husband. Or mockery, I'm not entirely sure yet which I will get, but that's the beauty of this sharing economy experiment. And indeed our marriage.

Caroline's house is large and her front garden is incredibly tidy. I look at her lawn as I wait for her to answer the door and wonder what she would think of the buttercup lawn we had in our old house. I used to call it 'rewilding' but our neighbours clearly didn't approve. Caroline appears and is as tidy as her garden, with very long, champagne-coloured nails, which I wouldn't associate with a keen cyclist – but if she's happy to part with her bike for three weeks at a time maybe she isn't *that* keen. Anyway, she's perfectly nice and wheels the bike out of her garage, looking at me as dubiously as I am looking at her. Maybe she's trying to work out if I am a Bike Person. Maybe she's wondering why my nails are so short. Who knows? The bike is also immaculate, which concerns me, but it also looks like quite a good bike, although I don't know much about bikes, so this probably doesn't mean much.

I put it in the back of the car with her help, and mutter something about a helmet as an excuse for not actually riding it away. Which immediately makes me think: I don't have a helmet, and we're meant to be going on a Family Bike Ride when I return. Back home, as I wheel the bike up the front path, my husband appears in the doorway, having clearly read my mind, waving a helmet at me. Well, he has *partially* read my mind, as this isn't quite what I envisaged. It's a child's bike helmet (which fits me, rather oddly – I didn't know I had a small head), and it is shaped to give the appearance of the wearer's head being eaten by an (admittedly not very realistic) shark, complete with fin on the top. 'It's the only spare one we have', says my husband, smirking.

Phoebe is keen to come too: she's been doing Bike Club and wants to show off her skills. Jake is playing some video game about the Mongol Empire and 'isn't fussed'. I feel nervous as we push our bikes down to the Meadows – the cycle paths there always seem quite hectic, in fact as a family we call them the 'psycho paths'. But that's where I will be cycling for the first time in twenty-five years, it seems. I look down at the handlebars and there are twenty-four gears. Twenty-four? My bike in Oxford had three. I suddenly can't remember which one is high and which one is low. I'm starting to panic but don't want Phoebe to notice in case she gets nervous too. Next thing, we're on the path, and there are other cyclists coming, including Deliveroo riders on electric bikes, going pretty fast. There are also some people who have attached tight ropes, the loose ones (not sure what they're called, loose ropes?) between trees, and are balancing on them – from where I am, they look just like collateral damage in the making. 'Go!' shouts my husband, so I get on and pedal and . . .

I can do it. I cycle off down the path, with barely a wobble. So it *is* true what they say. Phoebe is between us and doing great, and we zoom across Middle Meadow Walk in the direction of Holyrood Park. Then disaster strikes and my husband's chain comes off. He pulls over and tries to fix it, but 'something's up', so he tells me and Phoebe to go on by ourselves, clearly a bit disappointed, having waited the entire time we have been together to cycle along next to me. Phoebe seems up for carrying on, so we do, and apart from a few 'looks' due to the shark helmet, and one fall, it is incident free. The fall was Phoebe, not me – she recovered quickly, partly due to a nearby bagpiper (which does actually happen here), playing such a chirpy tune she burst out laughing and shouted at him, 'Play something sad, I just fell off!.'

We make it to Holyrood Park but don't attempt anything as steep as what I imagine my husband would have had in mind. On the way back, Phoebe draws level with me and we race, laughing manically. The cold wind whooshes in my ears and the walkers and runners pass in a blur. Back home, pink cheeked and smiling, I am exhilarated. My husband looks up from fixing his chain in the hall, and I burst out with a garbled stream of consciousness: 'That was so fun you can go really fast I loved it we did a race Phoebe fell off but she's ok when you fix your chain can I go for another ride with you???.' He smiles more than when Marley sat on his foot. A lot more.

———

Now for another kind of space sharing: park sharing. Sounds weird but bear with me. The sharing economy for parking allows people with their own driveways or parking spaces to rent them out to anyone wanting to park their car, or motorbike (or any other vehicle, presumably). What's the benefit, you may well ask? Well, for the person with the driveway, it means they can make money from this 'asset' when they're not using it themselves – that's standard sharing economy stuff and good news, especially in these cash-strapped times. But for the people looking for a parking space, it's good news too, as it means the chance to find off-street parking spaces in cities – some of which have charging points for electric vehicles to boot – quickly and cheaply, without driving around slowly or 'idling' while looking for a space, which as we know from talking about car sharing is a major cause of congestion and emissions. You can save money on petrol too, as well as avoiding a bit of stress. It's also safer, as you know how distracting it is when you're looking for a space: we've all seen (or been) that driver going at ten miles an hour and clearly not paying attention to anything other than finding somewhere to park. Commuters can book the driveways for long periods of time too, for example by the month: it's not just 'by the hour' parking. So all in all, these apps get cars off roads more efficiently and make use of existing city infrastructure to do so.

I register with a parking app: there are several available in Edinburgh, and these days the same goes for cities all over the world. Even though I live pretty near the centre of town, there is still reason occasionally to drive to another part of Edinburgh, where the parking is indeed both hard to find and expensive. In fact, the following week I am due to meet my friend Frankie for a gallery trip – Frankie is my art gallery friend, which sounds pretty middle-aged, but I'm fine with that. I studied art history, so I quite like wandering about galleries nodding at sculptures and calling them things like 'eloquent' and 'biomorphic' – and Frankie is actually an artist herself, so she's happy to join in. But mainly I like the gallery shops – and of course the cafés, because gallery cafés often do good cakes. My art history tutor would be so proud, I must mention him in the acknowledgements.

I digress. The gallery in question is quite near the centre of town, so I could walk, but it's on the other side of the centre to me and about thirty minutes, plus my Couch to

5K Ankle is playing up. So, without further justification for driving, I decide to use the sharing economy and cheaply rent someone's driveway to park near the gallery. On logging in, the app asks me 'What do you want to do today?' Erm – look at sculpture and eat cake? Once I've selected that I want to find a parking space, what's quite handy is that I then put in the place I'm going and it helps me find a space near that, also telling me how long it will take to walk there from said space. There's a driveway not five minutes from the gallery, and I can park there for a mere £2, compared to a lot more on the street. The rest of the booking just feels like a regular parking app, with the usual times and car registration number, the only difference being that I get a chirpy message from the homeowner thanking me for renting their driveway, with directions to the space. It's admittedly not as exciting as renting a handbag shaped like a hatbox but that's the sharing economy for you: just like life, it's not always glamorous, but it (usually) makes sense.

So where did this idea come from? I ask Rob Brown who is the co-founder of a sharing economy parking app called Kerb, which originated in Australia. He tells me that it didn't take an app for people to realise that their driveways could be a sought-after commodity. 'Before smart phones formalised anything like this,' he explains, 'homeowners with driveways near big stadiums like Wembley in the UK or Eden Park in Auckland knew they could cash in on what they had. They'd send their kids out to stand on the driveway, with a big cardboard sign saying 'Park here for £10'. The kids would probably get a cut but they wouldn't have to stand there for long. And although the homeowners made up their own prices, it regulated itself – if anyone asked for too much, nobody would park there. All technology has done is facilitate and enhance this – it's made the peer-to-peer transaction easier. That's where these parking apps have come from. We're all inspired by the same story and our technology just makes it possible for anyone to take part, and not just at big events – any time.'

I set off for the gallery leaving a bit of extra time for traffic issues, which I inevitably need due to driving the wrong way around the one-way system, but I won't bore you with more tales of my sub-standard sense of direction. I do, however, thanks to Google Maps, find the driveway I've booked fairly easily: it's on a street of 1930s pebbledash bungalows, and, as per the instructions emailed to me, the space is in front of a white garage. I drive in, feeling slightly uncomfortable, and try not to look through the net curtains to see if anyone is watching me and/or judging the bird poo on Cumulo Mumbus. Now, at this point, I'd like to relate a hilarious parking app incident that took place but – and I think this is important as it shows you that some types of sharing are not in fact fraught with challenges – no incident whatsoever occurred. Unless you count that when I arrived at the gallery, I saw that there is a car park, which was not only pretty much empty, but free. And also not five minutes' walk away. 'THERE WILL BE NO MIRACLES HERE' proclaimed the giant sign made of fairground lights on the front lawn of the gallery (by the artist Nathan Coley since you ask). No, indeed there will not.

———

While we're on cars, let's go back to Cumulo Mumbus, which, in spite of the bird poo, is feeling a lot better after a trip to the garage. They even mended the wing mirror, and cleaned up the inside, which is both pleasing and also embarrassing, considering what a state it would have been in. I wonder how they decided what was to be kept, and what should go in the bin. They left a small pile of 'items' on the passenger seat, including a Brad Paisley CD (my husband's) a book called *The Little Book of Sass* by Jonathan Van Ness from *Queer Eye* (Phoebe's), a pencil sharpener shaped like the Infinity Gauntlet (Jake's) and a Bergamot Calming Facial Spritz (mine). I worry about what they had to throw away. There would have been quite a lot of food, and possibly another snail. We might need to never go back to that garage.

Anyway, in light of the 'glow up' that the car has had, I decide this is the perfect time to try listing it to see if anyone would want to 'share' it. For the purposes of research, I choose a different platform to the one I used to borrow the Vauxhall Corsa. This one promises me that if I share my car when I'm not using it I could 'earn an average of £442 per month*'. I follow the website page down to find the other asterisk, where there is a lengthy explanation of how they got to the sum of £442. It sounds wholly unachievable for Cumulo Mumbus and indeed at the end of the paragraph it says 'Actual earnings may vary'. And I suspect that they will.

I choose 'Get started' and the website cheerily says 'Welcome back', even though I have no recollection of using this site before. Has Cumulo Mumbus been trying to rent *itself* out? Maybe it's trying to find a family that doesn't think snails are an OK thing to keep on your back seat. Once I've registered, I'm told that the process will take ten minutes, which is fine, and that I'll need the car registration number, which is not fine, but I can go outside and have a look. It also tells me that 'Guests need to see your car before they book it. Don't worry about this yet – we'll coach you on taking high quality photos later'. A few issues here. First – *guests*? That sounds fancy. I'm not sure anyone who has accidently sat on an M&S samosa wrapper in our passenger seat has thought of themselves as a guest before. Second: *coach*? How bad at taking photos do you think I am? Actually, don't answer that, I've just remembered what happened when I tried to find one of me and my in-laws' late dog. Third: I don't like being told not to worry. It makes me worry.

And worry I should, as on the next page there are lots of questions that I don't even understand, like 'Has your car ever had a branded or salvage title?' (which sounds kind of cool) and something about an 'odometer'. After some googling, I manage to fill in the first page, and move on to details about me. I upload my default smiley profile picture, then enter all the usual stuff like address and driver's licence. Next I'm asked 'What is your primary financial goal for sharing this car?' Tricky. I'm more interested in seeing if anyone will actually rent it out, to be honest – 'goal' seems a bit ambitious to me. I choose 'Not sure yet', then it asks me how often I want to share my car, and thankfully there is an option that says, 'I'm just curious'. I wonder if that's what Cumulo Mumbus chose when it went through this application on its own?

The final section is about the car itself and first involves an array of features with check boxes next to them, most of which I can immediately see I will not be checking. I scroll past Sunroof, Heated seats, Bluetooth . . . desperate to find any that I can say yes to. I don't know what 'All wheel drive' is but I'm hoping all of the wheels are involved when I'm driving, so I check that. I also check 'Child seat' because well, children sit in it, and I am desperate. It gets worse: in the next part, I have to 'Tell guests what makes your car unique and why they'll love driving it'. The thing is, I don't really love driving it, it's just a car. Don't get me wrong, when Heart FM is on and the sun is shining, as long as I'm in a 30mph zone, it's not unpleasant. But that's about it: for me it's very much something that gets me from A to B. So I make something up about it being a 'roomy family car' that's 'easy to drive' and move quickly on to the next section, ignoring the 'tip' that says that 'Listings with descriptions of at least 100 words are up to three times more likely to get booked'.

Then comes the 'coaching'. The website tells me to take 'beautiful, aspirational' photos of my car, and advises against anything 'lacklustre'. I feel cheered by their use of the word 'lacklustre' just because it's a good word, but then am immediately put off by their request that I find a 'scenic location'. I was just going to go out into the street and take the photos on my phone. I'm also warned against 'strange angles' which are apparently 'unsettling'. They are indeed: I remember this from my photo shoot for the fashion sharing app in the front garden, which made me look jowly. Can cars look jowly, I wonder?

Pondering this, I drive round to the other side of the Meadows and position the car so that there is just grass in the background, as opposed to the food recycling bin that it was parked next to on our street. I take the required six photos (minimum), including 'interior pictures so your guests know where they will be sitting'. I am hoping that any potential guest will know that they will be sitting in the seats without seeing a picture of them – but it's good to be clear, I suppose. Once I've uploaded the photos, entered my bank details for 'payouts' and agree to keep the car clean, which is in retrospect probably the hardest part of this process. I'm done. Let's see if Cumulo Mumbus passes the sharing test.

———

What other kinds of space sharing are there? A growing sharing economy trend is for peer-to-peer storage, which involves using a platform or app to rent out space you have in your home – such as a basement, garage, attic or even a spare room – for other people to store their stuff in. The advantage for the sharers is that they can make money from, well, nothing – and unlike Airbnb they don't need to change the sheets or make breakfast. For the sharees, it's a chance to access storage space nearby for a fraction of what a traditional storage company might charge.

As for the benefits, using space that already exists means that precisely no additional energy goes into the running or maintenance costs of the storage space. And the storage space is already built, while a purpose-built facility has already created its own carbon emissions just by being constructed. As well as this, in most cases, the space in your neighbour's home will be fairly conveniently located, cutting down on travel time and petrol usage, whereas self-storage units are often on the outskirts of towns and cities.

I'm intrigued, and although I have no space to offer – and as I mentioned before, all of our extra stuff (crap) is stored for free in my mother's garage. But for research purposes, I investigate storage space sharing platforms that operate in Edinburgh, and I'm pleased to see there are actually a few that do. Perusing the listings, I see it's quite a mix, from Danielle's spare room to Ekrem's garage, and Steve's basement to Macaria's loft. Some are 'padlocked', some 'dry lined' while others are 'dust free' or even (and this just sounds like boasting) 'completely mouse-free'. It does all seem very reasonably priced, though, and a quick cross-reference with a self-storage website shows that to be very much the case.

What else can you rent out the space in your home or garden for? Here are a few more brilliant ways the space sharing economy can work. It can help you offer the space in your garden for other people who don't have an outside plot to grow their own vegetables, like an allotment. Because allotment waiting lists are so long, especially in urban areas (as long as forty years, I find out), this can mean you get the chance to grow your own food sooner without waiting, and the whole concept uses under-used space, and promotes urban regeneration to boot. If you do have outside space, it's not just gardening that you can rent it out for.

There are also platforms that connect those with large gardens with people who want to have an outdoor event, wedding or show – or even to camp or park their motorhome. If you are lucky enough to have a swimming pool, there are even platforms that will help you rent that out too. Turns out space, even though it's a lack of something rather than a thing itself, can be shared not just for work, but for car parking, storage, horticulture, entertainment, the arts . . . even our holidays. And by doing so, we connect with not just the nearby spaces themselves, but the people that own them. In other words, our community, actual people around us, helping us to do something we maybe couldn't normally for less, doing something positive for the environment in many cases – and making some money for themselves into the bargain. If that's not the sharing economy in a nutshell, I don't know what is.

———

It's time for another of those film-style montages, so picture me using the workspace sharing app (but not accidentally crashing another meeting), and a park sharing app, with a few shots of me walking Marley, and collecting a Magic Bag here and there. I'm not sure what the music would be to accompany a sharing montage, it's not quite the same as a training montage, so something a bit less hectic than 'Eye of the Tiger'? You choose. In the meantime, a few space sharing practicalities: first, to be on the sharer (rather than sharee) side, you of course need to have space to rent out. As we live in the city, we don't have a lot of that going spare so, and this is the case with all platforms, sometimes, like me in this instance, you are only going to be on one side of the transaction. Which is fine. I don't have a driveway (we have an on-street permit), or a garage, a basement, a big garden . . . the list goes on. Before it starts to sound like I live in a badger's sett, which I categorically said I would not be doing in the introduction to this book, don't worry. It's just city life, and space is a commodity. Which is another reason why these platforms and apps are such a good idea: they really do share out the space that's available. It just so happens that Chez Tucker, it's in short supply. So I will, for now, be a space sharee and not a sharer.

Booking seems to be very easy, whether that's on a workspace sharing website, a storage sharing platform or using a parking app. The parking apps are particularly straightforward, just like using a 'regular' parking app – there just isn't as much choice. This will change, hopefully, as these types of app become more mainstream, which goes for all the other ones too. The workspace sharing app probably has the most choice, and quite frankly, I can't see myself ever not using this, it's such a brilliant alternative to having a permanent office for someone like me.

I wouldn't say that space sharing makes me feel as if I'm doing something positive for the planet – there wasn't quite such a 'warm glow' in that respect. But I do get that there are some environmental benefits, which we talked about before. There's a sense of community, too – the driveway owners connect on the app and send a 'thank you' message, and the workspace sharing app that I'm using is actively building a new community function so you can meet other users and network locally. Obviously, you still have to spend some money when you're space sharing. But a workspace is often free, depending on the app (although you might want to buy a drink or something to eat when you're there) and car park sharing is a lot cheaper than 'normal' parking. So is the storage space sharing, as I found out when I researched it, although I don't have a need for that at the moment (thanks, Mum).

As for the downsides, the main one would probably be that you might not be able to find exactly what you want near you: the perfect workspace, or parking space, or storage place, or garden or whatever space you need. That's peer-to-peer, though: in a way we've been spoilt by always being able to find the right thing straight away. And the thing is, without this sounding like a rallying cry (but also, I actually don't mind if this does sound like a rallying cry), the more we all do it, the better it will be. There will be more choice, more community, more money to be made – or saved. It will work for all of us. And it will work for the planet. Doesn't that make you want to give it a try?

A room with a (re)view

When I was almost ten years old, we went on a family holiday to Tuscany. It was the 1980s and this was considered pretty exotic, but back then a lot of things were, like kiwi fruit and that toy called Simon which was essentially just a frisbee with four coloured lights on it. This was my first time abroad: we flew to Pisa and stayed in a resort nearby, with a wide beachfront *viale* lined with shops selling ice cream and Italian leather goods. In the evening, we'd all shower off the sand and head out from our hotel for a *passeggiata* along the front. It seemed like another world, and one that I liked very much: the chattering of Italians around us and the balmy air smelt to me of promise, of possibility – a feeling that, although I didn't know then, I would have at the start of many evenings ahead of me.

On one of these evenings, my parents bought me and my sister a pair of sandals each from one of the stalls. They were made in front of us, and by made, I mean that we both chose a pattern of plaited leather, two interlinked strips of which were then hammered onto a pre-made wooden sole. I'd chosen a slightly sparkling bronze colour theme for my leather, and the sole had a small heel. I also remember that the man making them called me *biondina* and touched my hair. But although hastily made and, in retrospect, by someone fairly creepy, to me these sandals were like being handed the keys to the City of Adulthood. Maybe that's why I liked the rented stick of rock shoes so much. I clip-clopped back to the hotel with my parents and sister that night, ready to leave the first decade of my life behind me.

I don't remember much else about the holiday, apart from snippets from the beach, a visit to Florence (we saw Michelangelo's David, I was unimpressed/confused by his penis), and a coach trip to Pisa. My mother wouldn't climb the tower because she hates heights but we waved at her from the top part, which is no longer accessible to the public. I also recall that the head waiter at our hotel was a huge Rolling Stones fan, and got talking about the band to my parents, much to the disinterest of me and my sister. When my mother mentioned that she had seen them at Cheltenham cinema before they were famous (which is true, in 1962), the waiter nearly passed out with excitement, as only Italians can. For the rest of the fortnight, she was given five-star treatment in what was probably only a three-star hotel: doors were held open for *La Signora Rollinstones*, and my mother, a woman of only 40, who'd just found out her husband had early-onset Parkinson's, knew what it was to be famous, if only for a few days.

So holidays help. They heal, they restore, they inspire. But are they always good for the planet, and for communities? There's the rub. Our holiday to Italy was in the heyday of the package holiday: a travel agency had popped up near where we lived in Oxford and pre-internet, this was the only way you could get hold of the glossy brochures featuring bikini-wearing models basted in suntan oil, and be tempted by the 'sun-soaked beach escapes' that had become the essential family fortnight in the summer holidays, thanks to cheaper air travel.

Yes, we had all started going abroad on holiday, and the biggest downside of this in terms of carbon footprints is the travel itself. But where we stay is important too: accommodation is responsible for a massive chunk of the CO_2 emissions related to tourism. Research by the UN Environment Programme shows that globally, the tourism industry's consumption of resources – energy, water, land and materials (fossil fuels, minerals, metals and biomass) – is growing at the same pace as its generation of solid waste, sewage, loss of biodiversity and greenhouse gas emissions. 'In a "business-as-usual" scenario, tourism would generate through 2050 an increase of 154 per cent in energy consumption, 131 per cent in greenhouse gas emissions, 152 per cent in water consumption and 251 per cent in solid waste disposal. This is why sustainability must now define tourism development in the twenty-first century'.[11]

So sustainable tourism isn't just nice to have – we need it. The big question is, how can we swap, borrow or rent travel and holidays – and what are the benefits if we do? Well, there are actually quite a few ways that the sharing economy

11 www.unep.org

can be used to make tourism not just more sustainable, but better for other reasons – and I'm going to explore a few of them for you here. First, a quick reminder that in this book, we're talking about just the sharing economy, which isn't a cure-all, but one way we can help.

Let's start with home sharing. This means that instead of staying in a hotel, you share someone's home. In other words, you rent out a room in someone's house or apartment, while they're living there, and they 'host' you. So their home effectively becomes a hotel. It's perfect sharing economy, in a way: you have a 'thing' – in this case the place you live. Your 'thing' is not used all the time (a spare room, a couch, your Wi-Fi, your bathroom). Someone else has a need for what you have and by accessing it, saves money, and is able to do something they might not otherwise have been able to do. And you make some money out of this act of sharing too.

Aside from convenience, and money, what's the point of doing this? Well, from the perspective of sustainable travel, by staying in someone else's home, you join in with their usual use of energy and water, and their creation of waste – whereas in a hotel, you are part of a huge system of room cleaning, towel washing and plastic bathroom toiletry miniatures. Of course, it's not that simple, as we will discover later in this chapter, but the same could be said for most things, couldn't it?

In the spirit of that complexity, there is something else to add here about another type of home sharing that is unrelated to travel and tourism. It deserves a mention not least because it's such a good idea. This method of home sharing connects people who might need a bit of help to live independently in their own home with those who are in need of somewhere to live. So the homeowner gets live-in support and companionship, and the home sharer gets affordable accommodation, and in many cases, a rewarding connection (and often friendship) with someone who could be from a different generation or background. In western cultures particularly, we have moved away from the idea of living with multiple generations in the same home, and this not only revives that tradition but makes the most of under-used space.

Back to the travel version of home sharing. Like many of us, I've used Airbnb – in fact, before I started this sharing experiment, it was the only sharing economy platform that I *had* used. But the way I've used it has always been like any other booking site, to rent cottages or apartments for family holidays, either for a week or two, or sometimes for a couple of nights away in a city. These were homes, yes, but were they homes that we were 'sharing' with the owner? No. And were they homes that were even ever used by the owner? Doubtful – most of them had the feel of a holiday let, rather than a second home, let alone an actual home. So in that sense, it was no different to using any other booking site, or a holiday company.

What I'm going to do is use Airbnb for its original purpose, and that is renting a room in someone's home. The timing is perfect for this: the days are getting slightly longer, the last of the snow has thawed (hopefully: it can still snow at Easter as we all know) and I have some meetings in London coming up – so I've decided to come out of hibernation and have those meetings in person. However, my beloved Aunt Virginia, who I usually stay with when I'm in the capital, has a houseguest so can't put me up. I might normally have asked my very old friend Fiona (she's not old, our friendship is), or booked a hotel . . . but not this time. Instead, let the 'real' home sharing begin.

———

I already have an account on Airbnb but when I search this time, I don't choose the filter that I usually do which says 'Entire place', and instead I go for 'Private room', which adds, 'Your own room in a home or a hotel, plus some shared common spaces'. This is how you bring up the homeshare options, in other words rooms in people's homes. Airbnb isn't the only platform that does this of course, and you might prefer to choose another, so I've put some ideas in the summary at the end of this section. Back to my search: I pick the south-west of London, as I want to be quite near Aunt Virginia so I can meet her for lunch – and also not too far from the West End, which is where my meetings are.

The search brings up quite a few results, and I sift through them. I'm not keen on 'Private room in Wandsworth' which doesn't actually show any pictures of the room itself, just some photos of buses and one of the London Eye. Another room, hosted by Nadine, has a shared bathroom, which I'm not that keen on, and a review that simply says 'DON'T BOTHER'. Then there's another listing with a row of rubber ducks as the 'hero' image, one of which appears to be dressed in bondage gear. That doesn't really say 'home from home' to me. Then I spot 'Quiet ensuite room' hosted by Ruth. The room is described as 'light and airy' and 'painted in neutral colours', and the photos actually show the room, not buses or bondage ducks. It looks very pleasant, and there's a balcony looking out onto a garden. Ruth even offers a bathrobe and slippers, 'for your use'. I'm sold.

The room is a fraction – actually about a quarter – of the price of a decent hotel in the area. Once I've booked it, for just one night, I introduce myself to Ruth using the messaging function on the platform, so she knows I'm a normal person, and not into, for example, duck bondage. I also let her know when I'm likely to arrive. I won't have time to go to hers first before a work dinner, so I message her to say I hope she doesn't mind if I reach her around 9pm. She doesn't mind, it seems, and gives me her phone number so I can text her in case I get delayed.

The following week, a faint feeling of spring in the air, I head south on the train, watching the temperature on my weather app rise as it always does, degree by degree, as we rattle into England, through Yorkshire, then south, into Cambridgeshire, then London. It's always warmer in the south: I miss that sometimes, having grown up in Oxford, but nobody lives in Scotland for the weather. And on murky days in early spring like today, there's not a lot of difference between north and south when it comes to the climate. At King's Cross, I message Ruth to let her know I'm in London, then immediately regret this, feeling that it's not very useful information and more the sort of thing I would text Aunt Virginia. So I send Aunt Virginia the same message. She texts me back asking why I called her Ruth, if I'm OK, and if I'm still on for lunch the next day.

On the tube, I mull over whether I am using Ruth as a surrogate aunt, despite never having met her, but then I wonder if that's what 'hosting' is all about, and perhaps she would like that? I notice in a lot of the home share reviews, people talk about their host: 'Joanna is lovely, she made me feel so at home!'. 'Aayansh gave me a super tour of the local area. He's such a nice person'. 'I love staying here as Ji-Soo's breakfasts are the best and she is so welcoming'. It's all quite . . . personal. That's the sharing economy, though, isn't it – a person-to-person thing? But collecting a tin of mandarins from someone's gate, or driving their Vauxhall Corsa is, on the personal scale, probably about a three. Sitting at their breakfast table and chatting: it's got to be an eight, right? Which leads me to my next deliberation: what if you just don't like the person? You have to grin and bear it, I suppose, especially if it's only for one night. Negative reviews always seem to be as non-specific (and non-host related) as 'DON'T BOTHER', such as 'Better bring earplugs' or 'OK but won't come again'. I certainly didn't see any reviews that said anything like, 'Susan just wasn't my kind of person' or 'John and I didn't really hit it off'. Is that because all hosts are nice people, otherwise they wouldn't be hosting? I'm about to find out, at least about one of them. Ruth, show me what you've got.

My work dinner is at Colbert on Sloane Square, and after dessert, I make my excuses and head outside to get a taxi. Ruth hasn't replied to my message earlier telling her that I have arrived in London, which makes me feel a mixture of slightly neglected, and also concerned about how firm the arrangement is. I message her again, trying to sound not quite as 'niece' as I did before, but also very clear about the arrangement. 'Hi Ruth, it's Elle, I'm staying at your home tonight. I'll be with you in about fifteen minutes.' I ponder whether to sign off with the smiling emoji with the pink cheeks, but decide that Ruth looks too mature in her profile pic for such frivolities. I decide on just 'Elle', then worry that I've said Elle twice, and she might think I'm one of those people who talk about themselves in the third person.

I put these concerns down to the wine I had at dinner and just send the text, then order a cab to Fulham.

At the address, which is a large terraced townhouse, there is no answer. I feel a rising panic as I am standing on the street in an area of London that I don't know very well, the worse for three glasses of Gavi. And it's dark. But I have kept my side of the arrangement, seeing as it is 9pm, if not a few minutes before. I text Ruth again, this time a more curt, 'I'm outside', to which I get an immediate reply: 'OK'. 'OK' as in, it's OK that I'm outside (it's not) or OK as in, you're on your way to answer the door? Thankfully, it's the latter, and Ruth appears in her dressing gown about thirty seconds later. She is apologetic about both the dressing gown ('I've been looking after my grandson today and I'm exhausted') and making me wait ('I was on the phone'). I am relieved: Ruth might not be quite Ji-Soo level yet, but she's certainly not the charlatan I thought she was a few minutes ago. She waves me through the house, which is large for one person, and shows me to my room. It's just like the photos, clean and comfortable, and I'm relieved when Ruth keeps her tour short as by now I'm also tired, despite how early it is. I tell her I have to leave quite early in the morning for meetings in town, and she promises not to let me sleep in, and says she'll give me directions to Fulham Broadway 'at breakfast'.

At 7am, I shower in my ensuite and then realise that my linen & Other Stories dress, which I rented for this trip (along with the Damien Hirst bag again as it got so many compliments), looks like a crumpled rag. I'm not sure where the iron is and I'm also not sure about wandering about the house in my bathrobe looking for it, so I decide to text Ruth. She replies 'OK' again, which is as ambiguous as her last message, but then texts again a few minutes later saying 'Come down to the kitchen'. Obediently, I follow the stairs down to a basement with a large round dining table, a navy blue Aga, and French doors out to a back garden. The room smells quite strongly of fish – not in an unpleasant way, but maybe a bit much for this hour of the day.

I see that Ruth is roasting salmon, tray upon tray of it, which she explains is for 'Meals on Wheels', in other words, food deliveries for the elderly and infirm. 'It's my turn this week,' she says, as she takes my dress from me and insists she irons it while I have some breakfast. I sit in my robe, hair wrapped in a towel, munching Alpen while Ruth irons, telling me she only accepts female guests 'who seem nice', so I'm glad I've passed this sharing economy test. We chat about whether it's best to leave the skin on salmon when oven cooking it, and she asks me about my meetings that morning, and what I do. I feel relaxed, at home, and you know what, Ruth does have something of the aunt about her, although not a patch on Virginia, of course. I've felt warm glows from the sharing economy before, but they've tended to be about helping the environment. This glow is about human connection, and I love it.

I finish my coffee. Ruth hands me my dress, which is beautifully ironed, and goes back to her salmon, giving me directions to Fulham Broadway station over her shoulder as she kneels in front of the Aga. I head up the stairs to get changed, and she calls out, 'I hope you'll come again!' Then, when I'm almost out of earshot, I hear her add, 'That's the bath mat you've got on your head.' I could be embarrassed about this but, in my defence, it is a very thin bath mat, and Ruth is very nice. So I just don't care.

———

Nobody has rented out Cumulo Mumbus. I'm trying not to take this personally but looking at the range of cars available locally on the app, I feel that ours may be the Marley of the selection. In other words, people would have to take the time to get to know it before appreciating it. But why would they when there are other, shinier looking ones available, the car equivalents of Aspen? Maybe this is the case with all sharing platforms – your thing has to compete with other things, which might just be more appealing. My melamine spoons and my (not exactly brand new) car clearly don't have the same appeal as the coquettish radishes or Jenny R's carpet cleaner. Maybe there should be a warning issued to potential sharers: 'Don't take it personally if nobody wants to rent your thing: other things are available, and they just might be a little bit better/tastier/cleaner/more stylish/well-behaved (delete as appropriate)'.

Which brings me to the ups and downs of car sharing. Clearly, there is competition: if you are renting out your car, the more people list, the more other cars there are for people to choose. And although this means that more people are using the app which can only be a good thing, it also means that your rather careworn Vauxhall Zafira might be further down the list than say, a shiny red Suzuki Swift. That said, if you do rent your car out, you could earn extra cash that could even cover the costs of running it or, depending on how often you rent it out, make you some extra cash too. As well as this, using a community car sharing app means that, aside from the environmental benefits we talked about before, you're also helping someone local who perhaps can't access a conventional rental car or needs a quick 'by the hour' way to get around.

As a renter, I found the whole process really easy and surprisingly cheap. I would definitely use it again in similar circumstances and choose it over traditional car hire, but I think as a family we use our car too much to switch to car sharing as an alternative to owning. However, car sharing could be a great substitute for having a second car or, for people who go for weeks without using a vehicle, it's an ideal way to have access to a car , without any of the regular outgoings like tax, insurance and repairs.

Another consideration is that finding a car nearby was easy for me as we live right in the city, but I'm conscious that this isn't the case for everyone: car sharing apps will need to become more widespread if people in suburbs or rural areas are to have the same amount of choice. I hope car sharing does become more popular. In cities where it is well established, walking and cycling is more common and overall car use is lower, which shows that car sharing has a knock-on effect of creating less car dependent, healthier ways of getting around.

I didn't just rent a car, of course, there was Caroline's bike, too. I was not prepared for how much I would love this. By using her bike, I got to experience cycling again and that 'try before you buy' side of the sharing economy in action once more. For someone who probably won't become a regular cyclist, peer-to-peer bike sharing is a good alternative to buying, storing and maintaining a bike of my own. It's like a slightly more formal version of regularly borrowing a bike from a friend, without feeling as though you're taking advantage, and you have more choice than being limited to just one kind of bike.

But for someone who is rather taken by the idea (yes,

that's me) it was a brilliant way to test it out. And now, shockingly, I'm actually shopping around for a bike of my own. In fact, there's a second-hand bike shop on the next street and to my husband's delight, I've found one that might be perfect for me there. I think cycling about Edinburgh might also, if I get a different helmet, make me look a bit Dutch. I'd like that.

———

Back to home sharing, and a bit about the history of it. The original idea of staying in someone's home, like most sharing economy ideas, isn't new. What makes it different, what makes it part of the sharing economy, is that something as old as letting someone stay in your house has become possible at scale, thanks to technology. How else, in the modern world where our physical lives have become so secretive compared to our online existences, would we be able to tell people that we had a room going spare?

I ask Melanie Backe-Hansen, a House Historian who specialises in how people lived in and used their homes over the centuries. She tells me:

'In the past, most of the kind of 'ad hoc' lodging arrangements that have similarities with the current Airbnb model were set up through newspaper advertisements and through land or property agents or solicitors. Historically most people rented their homes. This could vary from a stable ongoing arrangement for the more comfortable occupant with a regular income through to the poorer community who rented by the week, or those who rented rooms or simply a space to sleep on a nightly basis. There was also a range of lodging houses and temporary accommodation.

'People did rent other people's homes, but as a rental arrangement – such as rented rooms or a whole rented house for a short period – this could be people taking rooms in London for the social season or those who took rooms for travel, such as, in Georgian and Victorian times, visiting Brighton to go sea bathing or Bath or Buxton to take the waters.

'It's also important to remember that until the nineteenth century, travel was not only dangerous, but something that was really only for the very rich or the monarchy and aristocracy, or to undertake trade or participate in a war. After the industrial revolution, this changed, gradually, as more ways to travel arrived, such as trains, steamboats, and, by the 1920s, aeroplanes. Workers also began to have more days off than just Sunday and the occasional "feast day" and with the mass-production of cars, beach resorts became hugely popular, with holidaymakers in the UK heading to the coast, and in the US flocking to Florida and Atlantic City.

'But travelling still cost money, so by the 1950s, I discovered, teachers and professors who had longer holidays than most were trying to work out how to afford to get away for several weeks in the summer months. They used their academic connections to link up with staff at colleges and universities in other parts of their own countries, or even further afield, to swap their homes. This way, they only had to pay for the travel itself, and not accommodation. The idea grew outside academia, with printed catalogues showing available properties, and arrangements made by letter. By the 1980s, companies like HomeLink were appearing, so that when the internet arrived, it wasn't long until the first home exchange website appeared, IHEN (International Home Exchange Network), which launched in 1995.

In 2006, Kate Winslet and Cameron Diaz starred in *The Holiday*, which brought home swapping into mainstream popular culture.

'A mention here of Cuba, which is considered by many as the original 'home share' country, with locals being allowed by the government to let out rooms in their homes to make extra money long before the likes of Airbnb. And although prompted by a lack of hotels in the country, it remains a popular and cheap way to visit Cuba and sample local food and culture.

'With children and more to the point, mess, home swapping was never something I pursued as a family holiday. My tidier sister-in-law Laura did, however, start home swapping pre-internet, "with huge catalogues of listings and a machine that plugged into the TV to contact the homeowners. There was no copy-and-paste so I had to type out every offer." she tells me. "At least 40 each trip! We then sent the agreement forms and house photos, photocopied at a local printing press, by snail mail." She goes on to say:

'Before the online platforms and things like reviews and star-ratings, everyone was taking a bit of a leap of faith. But we weren't nervous about strangers moving in as we'd been in touch for several months before the swap, so we felt like we knew them. Home-swapping is based on mutual trust and you take care of their house hoping that they are doing the same in yours. We almost always swap cars and these days use each other's computers too.

'We did it at first because we wanted to travel but couldn't afford it. But then we fell in love with the home-from-home feel of it. We liked acting like we weren't normal tourists. There have been a couple of moments, though.

On a Sydney exchange, the grown-up sons let themselves in and out while we were staying in their parents' house, and once tried to climb in the bedroom window one night after a few too many beers . . . But that was just one out of nearly 60 home swaps (to date), and it's been a really positive experience on the whole. People are like us and take care of our home and belongings as we do theirs, and both parties are keen that their fellow exchangers have a good holiday in their home and country.

———

Then came Airbnb. They're the only sharing economy 'brand' I'm going to talk about in this book, mainly because they are so big that they have become a verb, like Google. I certainly use the name often enough when I'm explaining the sharing economy to people: 'It's like the Airbnb of handbags/driveways/horses/swimming pools/random item that's being shared.' But even though this gets the point across, I'm not a fan of the phrase, because it feels like Airbnb gets all the glory, and I'm not sure it should. In creating the biggest success story of the peer-to-peer model, the founders of Airbnb also created the first sharing economy monster, and I think describing it needs some space in this book.

The original idea, like so many, is simple. In 2007, Joe Gebbia and Brian Chesky were living together in San Francisco but struggling with the rent. Gebbia had an idea that could solve this, and emailed Chesky one day in the lead up to a design conference in the city. The subject line of the email was 'subletter' – such a casual idea that it didn't even warrant a capital 'S'. Gebbia suggested they put up conference guests on air beds in their apartment, as hotels were in short supply. That's where the name Airbnb comes from – in fact the original web address was 'airbedandbreakfast.com'. He signed off the email with 'Ha!'.

It took a couple of years, a lot of rejections from prospective investors, and a rebrand to 'Airbnb' to really get going – but around fifteen years later, Airbnb now has over six million listings worldwide. However, this growth has come at a price. First of all, the utopian ideal of letting out a spare room in your house, or a sofa bed or even an air bed, stopped being the norm, and the platform filled up with 'whole properties'. Which is fine, if you're renting out your house while you're away. But it moves a long way from 'sharing' if you're a landlord using the platform to list multiple properties that could be affordable housing for locals, or a tenant subletting their property, or someone letting an unsafe, unlicensed property or even a 'fake' property in an attempt to scam platform users. You get the picture.

And there's more: the effect on the cities where this style of letting has taken off. Airbnb has turned formerly residential neighbourhoods in cities and towns into tourist zones, disrupting the lives of locals, and keeping people awake at night with parties and the clattering of suitcases. Another thing: as appealing as the 'belong' ethos of Airbnb is, if you truly 'live like a local' then you cook your own meal at home, and don't have hotel staff turning over your room. No bad thing? In theory, but hotels actually employ local people, and restaurants in the tourist zone of a city do too, and are there to be eaten at. Yes, it's a cheaper way to travel, and yes, in some areas, 'short stays' like Airbnb can help local economies. But in big cities, with a wide range of regulated travel accommodation, whole properties let out by landlords (who are often listing multiple properties) can erode local communities and culture.

Housing problems can't just be blamed on Airbnb, though: a lack of housing, particularly affordable social housing, is part of the picture too. That said, in several countries, laws have been passed to lessen some of the negative impacts of Airbnb. This usually means requiring hosts to get a permit or licence, or at least register what they intend to do with their property. In many cities there is also a limit to the number of days in a year that you can rent out your property on the platform. In New York, the laws are particularly strict: you can't rent out a property you don't live in as holiday accommodation, and renting your home out to a tourist for fewer than 30 days (unless a 'permanent resident' is present during the entire rental) is also illegal. What's interesting is that the only way around this is to rent out private or shared rooms in a property that you are living in – and this takes us right back to that air bed on the floor idea, and the original ethos of home sharing.

All answers are confidential

I discovered recently that the dreams we have aren't as unique as you might think. In fact, I learned from some light googling that we're all pretty much having the same ones: we dream that our teeth are falling out, that we're being chased, that we're back at school sitting an exam, we're flying, falling, pregnant or driving an out-of-control vehicle. Sound familiar? It does to me: I feel like I have these dreams all the time, to the point of tedium, where I am considering switching to a different streaming service in my head.

The other dream I have on a regular basis involves going to the toilet, and it doesn't flush but instead starts to overflow. Having researched this dream extensively, I have discovered that, according to 'experts', it means that 'you have become too careless with your life of late – negligent, even'. And by 'you', they mean me. And by 'negligent', there are a lot of options here, but I think it's either to do with Jake's violent PlayStation games or the food hiding in the salad drawer. Or maybe the snail in the car. Anyway, plenty to work with.

My fear of overflowing toilets, no doubt amplified by this very dream, or indeed causing it, means I am unafraid to show up for a bit of amateur plumbing, should things go wrong with our own 'IRL' toilet. I will often refer to YouTube to get a household task done, with varying degrees of (OK, very little) success. My husband is less likely to fix something than he is to write a song about fixing something, so needs must. I have nearly mended the toilet a couple of times, and know my ballcock (snigger) from my floater (snigger snigger). I once even almost fixed the combi-boiler. When the plumber came, it turned out it was just a case of twisting a tap until it hissed a bit. So what if you need a professional only that briefly? And you don't want a £500 invoice at the end of it, especially if all that was necessary was twisting something until it hissed? Wouldn't it make sense if I could swap something I *did* know how to do with the knowledge of someone who knew that all you had to do was twist it until it hissed?

You might be wondering what particular branch of the sharing economy can help me out with this. Well, it's called skill sharing, and I am very excited to try it out, partly because I love the idea, and partly because I've done some ad hoc versions of it myself in the past, as many of us may have done, without necessarily noticing. Mine usually revolve around writing, so in the past I've helped a friend with the wording on her yoga website, and in return she gave me a one-to-one session. Our old neighbours used to often prune the trees in our garden because they had the right tools and I would bake for them because I like baking and I'm good at it (usually: I did have a run of dry sponges a couple of years ago, though, which has not been forgotten by my family).

It's swapping, it's just that the under-used asset, rather than being a physical one, is your skill. Unsurprisingly, this concept isn't new, but we'll get onto that later. What *is* new is the rise in sharing economy platforms and apps that allow cashless, time-based skill exchanges. The technology allows one hour of your time to equal an hour of someone else's, but you get a 'credit', so you don't have to trade your hour with the same person who used you, just anyone on the platform or app. For example, if you spend an hour walking someone's dog, you can exchange this for an hour of someone coming over to fix, for example, your toilet. Or mow your lawn. The point being that every skill is equal in value – it's the time that's the currency.

So where does the idea come from? Trading goods and services in exchange for other goods and services is age-old and is called 'barter'. I found out that it can be traced back to around 6000 BC in Mesopotamia, and then later Phoenicia and Babylonia, where people swapped labour for anything from weapons to tea, spices and salt. It was disputes that arose over the varying value of time and items that led to the creation of money. I also discovered that the first settlers in America used bartering to exchange things like wheat and the skin of male deer (where the word 'bucks' comes from), and also traded skills, like exchanging help fixing a roof for, say, help planting crops.

More recently, in 1980, a man called Edgar Cahn, who had been involved in American politics as a speechwriter for Robert F. Kennedy, created the concept of 'time banking', which he first called 'service credits'. It was at a time when money was in short supply for socially deprived areas in the US: 'Ronald Reagan was withdrawing funding for social programmes. They were closing down. I thought that if there was going to be no more of the old money to support communities, we should create a new one,'[12] Cahn said of his idea. The service credits were later named 'time dollars', and later still 'time credits' and 'timebank hours'. Cahn's idea grew into a global movement, and although the man himself recently died, his Timebanking legacy lives on, and has been revived in the last few years by just the kind of technology that we're talking about.

So what's the point in skill sharing? First, it's important to note here that because the under-used asset in this type of sharing is a skill, unless the skill is specifically environment-related, like doing a beach clean-up, for example, this branch of the sharing economy doesn't necessarily have the environmental credentials that we've seen so far. What it does have, in swathes, are community benefits. Skill sharing encourages individuals to form local connections, learn new things, interact with other people from different generations, cultures or backgrounds – and in doing so helps them to feel happier, healthier and less isolated.

But this isn't just about the intangible benefits: skill sharing is also a very practical choice to help save money, and in that sense can empower not just individuals but local businesses and community organisations. For example, if you are cash-strapped but need a little help with childcare, you can trade your own skills for an hour or two of help without having to spend actual money. And if you are a new business, you could trade web design for some bookkeeping. Or perhaps you might want to use skill sharing to road test

---

12 https://timebanks.org/

a new project that you don't feel confident enough to charge for yet, such as life coaching or business consulting. Skill sharing also gives you the chance to try things that you wouldn't normally, without any actual outlay – this is what I'll get into when I try it. And it democratises, too, something the sharing economy always seems to be good at: contribution is what's important on a skill sharing platform, so everyone is valued in the same way, whether they are there to offer you a lift somewhere or teach you a foreign language.

———

I register on a skill sharing platform and set up my profile. I'm getting pretty used to this, choosing a smiley pic, writing a snappy but approachable 'bio', which is usually something about being 'an Edinburgh mum of two' or 'passionate about [*insert type of sharing here*]'. At least on this site I don't have to find a picture of myself with a dog. And at least if I did, I now have plenty of me and Marley, who is surprisingly photogenic and not averse to a selfie. On the skill sharing site, I also have to say what 'skills' I'm offering – you can't just sign up and use other people's skills, that's the reciprocal nature of skill sharing that we talked about earlier – although you are usually given a couple of hours credit to get you started.

I ask Jake what skills I should list and he looks at me as if seeing me for the first time as a human being as opposed to just someone who provides him with meals and takes him to the orthodontist. 'Being a mum?' he suggests, brow furrowed. 'Mumming?' he adds, as if by creating a verb he has added value to his fairly useless suggestion. I ask Phoebe who looks equally confused. 'Fashion?' she says, which is more of a compliment than a suggestion, so in that sense it is appreciated. But I am no further forward.

After some thought, I go for 'Copywriting, PR and marketing services' which all feel like something I could probably do and also, importantly, condense into an hour at a time, which is essential when you are using hours as the units of currency. I also want to list skills that can be done virtually, which although not essential, will perhaps improve my chances of being booked. I also have to add a description of my services, say which days I am available, and, if I like, add an image to 'go with it'. I can't really think of an image that will add much to the offering so I just upload a picture of a desk, and hope that nobody thinks I make desks, in an hour. Over dinner, I tell my husband and suggest he lists a skill too. Somehow 'If they want me, they can pay me' sounds quite menacing with a Scottish accent. I change the subject.

Later, I browse the skills that I can use with my two hours' credit (and hopefully more credits when I am booked for my desk making, I mean copywriting). The range is quite impressive, and I'm immediately cheered to see that plumbing is available, which I make a mental note of for any future flushing concerns. 'Smoke Alarm Guidance' is equally practical, but I am uncharacteristically organised in that respect. What else . . . there's an hour-long 'Love Your Lymph' consultation, which is tempting, as is the 'Tummy Time' session until I realise it's for babies. I keep scrolling – and then I see it, the perfect skill to kick off with: 'Starting Your Own Wine Cellar'. Something that is realistically never going to happen, but how wonderful to get the chance to spend an hour talking about such a fanciful notion.

'Ever considered starting your wine cellar?' asks the description, written by a skill sharer named Adrian. Adrian, I'm going to have to say no, I haven't. 'I started with a small 12-bottle rack in my kitchen and now.......!' the description continues. I wonder what that extensive row of dots and an exclamation mark means – that he drank it all? This is definitely what would happen in my case. But I like the sound of his promised hour of 'advice which can be tailored around tastes, space and budget'. Which in my case consists of: taste (most wine, any colour), space (limited), budget (none). Whether or not Adrian can help me, an hour talking about wine is always an hour well spent, so I book my first skill share for after the Easter holidays.

———

The kids are about to be off school for two weeks and the weather forecast is good, so a break is in order. Of course, any getaway needs to be a sharing affair, but that doesn't necessarily mean home sharing: there are other ways to swap, borrow and rent to make your holiday better for the planet – and in many cases better for you and your community too. One way is camper van sharing. You might wonder how driving a giant vehicle around could be better for the environment, but bear with me. People who holiday without going abroad are not adding to the huge emissions caused by air travel, for one thing. And as well as that, just like car sharing, by sharing a motorhome you contribute to fewer new purchases of these big vehicles, which can produce more emissions while they are being made than they do in a lifetime of driving. Peer-to-peer camper van rental doesn't just cut down on the number of motor homes on the road, it also reduces the demand for new ones to be produced, lowering the environmental expense of manufacturing.

Then there are tents, which might appear, due to their lack of an engine, to be a much greener option. But unfortunately, they're seen by many people as disposable: around 250,000 tents are abandoned at music festivals each year across the UK alone, with many of them ending up in landfill, where the plastic they're made of can take 10,000 years to decompose[13] – what a charming archaeological find that would be for a future human. Thankfully, the sharing economy now allows you to borrow someone's tent when it's lying unused, rather than you having to buy one. And of course on a stuff sharing platform, you can rent a whole range of holiday-related equipment from your neighbours too, from car roof racks to picnic tables, and suitcases to surfboards.

My husband suggests camping. There's something in his look which is half delight, half challenge, as he knows – like we all do by now – that I'm not that 'outdoorsy'. In fact, camping for me has always been something that's part of my duty as a parent, rather than an activity I could really get stuck into. I mean, if I get that uptight about a toilet going wrong, how uptight do you think I get about there being *no toilets at all*. You're right: pretty uptight. But a gauntlet has been thrown down, and as the kids cheer, I can only join in, for fear of being the one who doesn't get as excited as everyone else. We head down to my mother's garage where all our 'big things' are stored, and after moving a few boxes

---

13 https://aiforg.com/

of Very Important Items like the kids' old school jotters, and debating who the travel cot belongs to (it doesn't matter, we'll never use it again – maybe we should rent it out?), we pile the tent in the back of the car. Once home, my husband and Jake put it up in the back garden, to see if it's still OK after the lockdowns, and it is – except now that the children have suddenly become giants, it's also clearly too small.

Of course we won't be buying a tent, that's not what we're doing at the moment. So enter tent sharing, stage left. Which I have to say, is a great idea. I mean how often do you use a tent – three or four times a year, maximum? And they take up so much room. Also, if we don't own one, it might mean we go camping less, but don't tell anyone I said that. On the tent sharing website I've signed up to, I immediately spot the filter that says 'Premium: arrive to a tent ready pitched and chill'. Well this sounds promising. Unfortunately, my husband's favourite spot for camping is so out of the way that there is little possibility of this service being available where we're going. To give you an idea, it's nearly the same distance north of Edinburgh as my hometown of Oxford is to the south of Edinburgh. I'm not kidding: Scotland is that big. And wild. And devoid of toilets.

Sure enough, the 'Premium' option seems to be available in places like Sussex, not Gairloch, which is an admittedly beautiful spot on the coast of Wester Ross, looking out to the Hebrides. Queen Victoria was a fan, apparently, so who am I to turn my nose up at it if she could get there in a horse and carriage. I choose 'Self-pitch (rent the tent and pitch it yourself)' and scroll through tepees, bell tents and domes, with some assistance from my husband who will realistically be the one responsible for putting it up. I will help obviously, but that usually involves standing there holding a thing until I am asked to put that thing down and then hold another, different thing. I'm good like that. A real catch.

We rule out anything that means we all have to be in the same room all the time. And by room of course I mean section of a tent, not an actual room. We haven't been camping with the kids since they turned into mini adults, and this means that firstly, they need some privacy, and that's fine – but it also means that they are now very annoying. I say this with love: they are meant to be annoying, they are teenagers (or nearly, in Phoebe's case). And we are meant to be annoyed by them most of the time, that's our job as parents. I read somewhere that it's called 'soiling the nest': they start being a pain in the arse so that you don't mind as much when they fly off. But they also get on well with each other, and they're very funny, so when we're not laughing *at* them, we are laughing *with* them, which generally makes them very good company.

All that said, it's essential for my husband and I to try to at least create *some* distance between us and them. Jake is currently obsessed with Elvis, which means he not only listens constantly to Elvis playlists (loudly, singing/shouting along), but also tries to do some of his famous 'moves', with varying degrees of success. He hurt his foot recently attempting the dance from *Jailhouse Rock* but I refused to take him to the doctor with an Elvis-related injury. Phoebe is best kept at arm's length at night as she is an enthusiastic sleep talker, and always sounds, not angry, but very forceful, shouting out things like 'NO THANKS' and 'THIS WAY PLEASE'. At least she's polite, I suppose.

I spot a 'Zenobia 6 man Hi Gear tent' which has 'nightfall bedrooms' (so you don't get woken up at daybreak by the light coming in) and a 'large living area with carpet for warm underfoot' (sic). Sounds almost comfortable, if slightly bad at grammar. I also like the fact that it says it's 'easy' to pitch and that it only takes fifteen minutes, which means only fifteen minutes of me standing there holding things. It's in Glasgow but we can collect it (from the owner, who's called Dougie) when we go to visit my stepdaughter, plus it's only £10 a day which is a lot cheaper than buying one. And we get that warm glow that comes from doing something positive, which will be handy when we're actually in the tent, as this is Scotland, and it's Easter, so we're not getting our hopes up about the weather.

———

The following weekend, with Cumulo Mumbus packed full of practical things like portable stoves (thanks to my husband) and Elvis memorabilia (thanks to Jake), we drive north, a bit more north, and then north again. The motorways end and are replaced by A roads, then B roads, then roads that take your breath away when you turn a corner, suddenly faced as you are by the kind of epic landscapes you normally only see in coffee table books. We had an early start, so reach the campsite, which is right on the beach among the dunes, at about 4pm. After a mainly sunny drive, my husband and I exchange glances at the bank of grey cloud sitting out on the sea, and looking like it is definitely not moving away from us. But he is from Highland stock and such clouds to him are barely an inconvenience. Besides, there's nowhere else to go, so it's time to see if the Zenobia really takes only fifteen minutes to put up.

We get it out of the car, in its khaki-coloured zip-up bags, and my husband starts emptying out huge bits of rolled up tent and poles and other items while muttering about how we should have just bought our own because of the bloody somethings being missing. I tune him out, watching the bank of cloud getting blacker and closer, and mulling over why they made the name of the tent sound so much like 'xenophobia'. The children help a bit, going off to 'see if the café is open' and 'find the loo' (please let there be loos) and other such activities that really mean 'avoid helping with the tent'. Phoebe has also announced that she 'doesn't want to sleep in someone else's stinky tent anyway,' which is surprising, as she's usually fairly easy-going, except when she's asleep. By the time we've laid it out and my husband has found the bloody somethings, which aren't missing (sorry Dougie for thinking that they were), a light drizzle has begun. According to my husband, this is not good because it means the inside of the tent might get wet. Oh good. The large living area with carpet which was the only thing keeping me going might end up being a large damp living area with a damp carpet. I start to feel nostalgic about Ruth's bath mat. At least it was dry, to start with.

By the time we are at the 'banging in tent pegs' stage of the pitching, which is probably about half an hour later and definitely not fifteen minutes, a storm is raging. Over the wind and rain, I can hear the children, who are back in the car, singing 'Suspicious Minds'. I long for the inside of the car: my hands have turned an odd shade of mauve as I clutch the pegs and poles and other tent things I don't know the name of, and my legs are doing a kind of involuntary shaking I last witnessed when I was in labour with Jake.

But my husband is on top of it, and as the tent rolls to one side in the wind, and then rolls back the other way, he runs round, tightening ropes, banging things and swearing profusely – and soon, we have a tent, and it is up, and this is where we must live for five days. Soaked with both rain and sweat, we unload the car of both our belongings and our offspring and set up the 'bedrooms'. By the time we've done that, the storm has eased, and a little patch of blue sky has appeared.

Most people have been camping, so I won't tell you what it's like. But there are toilets at the campsite, and they're quite clean, albeit a few minutes' walk away. The café is open too, and it serves pretty delicious seafood. We play a lot of cards, and a game called 'Dobble' which involves shouting and therefore everyone loves it. We even have Elvis Monopoly. On the third day, the sun comes out with a vengeance, and we inflate a dinghy that I didn't even know we had. The beach is glorious and pretty much deserted: pale sand dotted with purple jellyfish, stretching off towards a glittering sea. The children don't want to go in the dinghy: Jake has recently watched *Jaws* and then scared both himself and Phoebe with stories about it. My husband and I are more confident about the lack of great white sharks in the North Atlantic Ocean, so we throw ourselves in and paddle about in the icy breakers, laughing, the kids looking on bemused. But we know why. Life was on pause for two years, and now it feels like it's started passing even more quickly. It's unspoken, a need to take it all in, every sensation, in the hope that this will make us more ready to get old.

In the evening, a man on the table next to us in the campsite café asks if we're 'prepared for tomorrow'. We all look blank: there's no phone signal here so we don't really know about anything that's going on if it's not related to Elvis, or jellyfish, or the xenophobic tent, which is proving to be quite comfortable. 'The Big Storm,' he whispers, like some kind of prophetic sea spirit from a children's book. We did not know about this, no, strange-man-eating-scampi-and-chips. As we get ready for bed that night we notice there are fewer tents on the campsite, and caravans are driving away as Phoebe and I walk up to the toilet block with our washbags. But my husband is undeterred. 'We've come this far,' he says, but later I notice him standing outside the tent staring at the sea and frowning. I feel like I'm in some Victorian drama set on a lighthouse, or something similar.

The next day, we eat beans for breakfast perched on camping chairs outside the tent. 'This is the life,' my husband says, but I can see him glancing around at what is now an almost deserted campsite. He goes off to the 'office' to speak to the 'guy', and the camping chair that he was sitting on blows into the long grass. Jake retrieves it and Phoebe and I go and sit in the tent to watch *Pitch Perfect* on the laptop. The rain has started coursing down the plastic windows of the tent in rivulets and there's a smell in the tent that reminds me of Marley when we walk him in wet weather. We've hardly even got to Fat Amy's mermaid dance when my husband reappears, telling us to pack up. Scampi guy was right: a storm is coming, and Xenophobia is unlikely to survive it. And so, as the wind whips up again, we take the tent down, which is, Dougie, actually fairly easy, you are right. I think we did pretty well to last for three nights at Easter, but for the fourth and fifth, we check into a hotel in Aviemore. There's a pool with flumes, mini

Elemis products in the bathroom and haggis for breakfast, if you want it that is (I don't, ever: the kids say that's 'because of my Englishness'). Nothing is sharing economy about any of this, but sometimes you just have to get out of the rain.

———

After the camping trip, my husband returns the tent to Dougie, saying he hopes 'sharing economy people aren't fussy'. Later that week, Adrian the wine expert and I meet in a nearby café and delicatessen called Victor Hugo, which overlooks the Meadows and is a bit of an Edinburgh institution. It's also a busy and safe place to meet a man you don't know. That said, I have checked out Adrian's reviews on the platform of course, which are most complimentary: one even says that 'If you love wine, you will love this' so I feel that Adrian will be a) who he says he is, and not a potential murderer and b) knowledgeable, and worth crossing the Meadows at 11am on a Tuesday morning for.

This is probably a sensible place to talk about trust. It's one of the things that makes the sharing economy tick: because transactions are between two people, rather than between a person and a business, it's vital that there is trust there, and that the other person is who they say they are. That's why sharing economy platforms tend to have lots of checks when you sign up, like ID verification. And it's also why reviews are so important: the more people transact with an individual on a platform and like them, the more positive reviews they get. But these aren't just 'nice to have', they're a way for other users to make sure the person is trustworthy. So when you're using a sharing economy platform or app, check out the reviews of the person you're thinking of borrowing from or swapping with, and always leave reviews too, as this helps to build up a safe community and keep out what they call 'bad actors' (which always just makes me think of *Robin Hood: Prince of Thieves*, for some reason).

Back to my impending wine cellar. In preparation for the meeting, I have completed a questionnaire about my wine purchasing habits, which is a little embarrassing, especially as in answer to the question 'Where do you get your wine?' I initially put 'Deliveroo' without thinking and then tried to cross it out and put something more sophisticated, like 'My local independent wine merchant'. Sadly I had used one of Phoebe's glitter pens again and couldn't seem to hide the word 'Deliveroo', plus the printer had run out of ink so I couldn't print out the questionnaire again. Ah well, at least Adrian would know what he was dealing with ie, me, who gets wine delivered to my house at 6pm by a guy on a bike. In my defence, this does not happen every night and I often add something else to the order just so it doesn't seem so, well, you know. Like muesli. Muesli says I not only intend to get up tomorrow but I intend to be healthy when I do, even if it will all go downhill later. I'm fairly sure the Deliveroo rider doesn't even look at what's in the bag and/ or care, but it makes *me* feel slightly better.

Adrian is already at Victor Hugo: he looks just like you might expect a wine expert (red trousers, redder cheeks) and is warm and friendly. We greet and I hand him the questionnaire: he eyes the glitter pen writing with a look of pity mixed with concern and I am suddenly relieved it says at the top of the page that 'all answers are confidential'. We start talking about Italian wine, which he establishes immediately that I probably only like because I can speak

Italian and pronounce the names. I hadn't realised that and feel I have learnt something in the first five minutes, although mainly about myself. We move on, talking about what food I enjoy (all the food), what wine goes with it (any wine), and whether I would be willing to 'lay down' a wine (unlikely). It's actually all very interesting, and I find out a lot about how to store wine – and why – and which wines improve with age and which don't.

Then we get on to the cellar part. Adrian asks me if I had forty-eight bottles of wine, would I have a space where they could be stored? Well, Adrian, if I had forty-eight bottles of wine, the only explanation would be that I was having a party that night. And in terms of space, the answer is no, but I know a sharing economy app that could maybe help, and wonder how Ekrem would feel about me storing forty-eight bottles of Vouvray in his garage. I could ask, I suppose.

———

Later, my wine knowledge well and truly expanded, I summon Deliveroo, order some 'muesli' and go back to the skill sharing platform. I have one more 'free' skill sharing hour to use so I have a look at what else I can redeem it for. There really is quite the range, from life coaching to practical stuff like something to do with 'setting up Asana', which I assume to be yoga related until I google it. There's also 'Dove Release'. I wonder if I have a suitable occasion coming up to warrant this. I try to picture calling the family through at dinner time for one of my regular risottos. (You know the ones that have shifted so far away from the original Italian recipe that Gino D'Acampo would put a horse's head in your bed. Anyway, we all like it, devoid of Parmesan and butter as it is.) And so the children would come in and sit down, the garlic bread would be passed around the table and lo – a word I never thought I would use in this book – white doves would fly out from a Le Creuset dish, making a wonderful spectacle that would brighten up a midweek meal no end. The reality of course would be that a) I would hide in the hall cupboard as I hate flapping things in small spaces and b) the family would think I had finally lost my mind, especially after the carpet cleaner expedition and the toilet chairs.

I decide against Dove Release and instead investigate 'Burlexercise', which I feel less drawn to, perhaps because of the women wearing feather boas holding dumbbells in the picture. These seem like two things that don't go together at all. But Natasha, the instructor, promises it's a way to 'destress and feel awesome' and says she is a coffee lover who is 'desperate to get a cat'. Maybe she can come round and take the one that keeps wandering around our house like it owns it? I read a bit more and find out that Burlexercise is a fitness/dance combination designed to 'burn calories, tone and make you feel more confident'. After all that banana bread, I'm in, so I book the next available online session for the following Monday.

The day comes and by 5.30pm I'm not really feeling very 'nipple tassel' so hope that normal clothes will suffice. Having done a few online workouts over lockdown I do have something that passes for workout gear – but only to me, covered as it is in either holes, sweat stains or both. I try to find something that looks like I am used to exercising in public but the only combination that works is completely black and makes me look more like a middle-aged mime artist than a burlesque dancer. I am also slightly concerned I will have to hold my stomach in for the entire hour – that's right, HOUR – of the class, which I know is what you're meant to do anyway when exercising (something about your core) but an hour seems like a long time – I'm more used to doing it for say, a photo. I'm also worried about my Zoom background: I'm used to creating professional-looking ones for work calls or presentations but this is different, as it needs to show my whole body. I thought this was meant to be a 'de-stressing' experience, not a 'stressing' one.

I arrange my laptop artfully on the mantelpiece just in time for the class to start. We all say hi, then Natasha gives us the option to turn off our cameras 'if we prefer', although you can tell she'd rather we left them on. I am tempted but it's not really in the sharing spirit. Someone called Ava turns hers off. I wonder if Natasha will remove her, Jackie Weaver style. The woman left (there are only four of us, including Natasha) looks like she's about 20 and possibly a swimwear model. We start our warm-up with some dancing and I begin to feel this is going to be a long hour, having last danced in public in the nightclubs of the 1990s, and then not dressed as a mime artist (to my knowledge – they were pretty wild times). Slowly, I start to get into it: some of the moves are quite 'Charleston', some are more 'salsa', and I briefly lament the fact I never bothered to get into *Strictly*. Then I notice that Natasha can't actually see my feet so I concentrate more on waving my arms about in the right way, holding my stomach in and wishing I was the swimwear model.

Suddenly it's halfway through, and I realise that the time has flown by and I have a shiny glow last experienced when I checked on some oven chips. Natasha then tells us to 'move onto the floor' making me wonder for a minute what she thought I have been on up to this point. I see she means that I should lie on a mat, which I don't have, so instead I use the best towel I have, which I recently borrowed from a hotel, and reposition the laptop accordingly. I don't have time to check my background as we're straight into the ab and 'booty' work, which is like a regular workout but with some burlesque flourishes. Natasha soothingly tells us that if we need to make modifications, we can, which I guess is aimed at me, not the swimwear model, who seems to be romping through it. I'm now pretty red in the face and as I attempt a side plank, with an empowering sexy arm wave, I notice on the screen that not only is my tongue sticking out of the corner of my mouth in concentration, but that Henry the Hoover is smiling beatifically behind me. With Freddie Mercury's *The Show Must Go On* blaring from Natasha's Spotify, the whole scene looks less burlesque and more like a cry for help.

———

Back to travel and holidays. Before we get on to the pros and cons, here are a couple of unusual ways the sharing economy supports travelling. The first is crowd shipping. Yes, your journey somewhere could be an under-used asset: the cornerstone of a sharing economy transaction, if you have space in your luggage or vehicle. In other words, rather than use a courier or traditional shipping company to send an item, somebody could use you, because you're going that way anyway. This type of platform connects people to travellers who have space in their luggage, tasking them with bringing back items from abroad for a fee. This can just be something that might cost a lot to ship, or a product from an in-person store that can't be bought online. It doesn't have to be abroad, either – some apps connect you to travellers going by train or car to take a parcel in the same way. This feels like the 'real' version of sharing economy delivery, compared to the on-demand delivery apps that like to call themselves sharing economy – because it cuts down on unnecessary journeys rather than creating new ones with a new set of emissions into the bargain.

You can also find apps that allow you to book somewhere to store your luggage – this one crosses over with space storage. The concept isn't strictly peer-to-peer either as it tends to use businesses like shops and hotels, unless there are some that allow you to rent out space in your home for the purpose – but it does make the most of under-used space so is worth a mention. What else? You could borrow or swap someone's boat, without or without skipper, depending on your sailing abilities, or you could borrow someone's vintage car to drive you from the airport to your villa, if that's your cup of tea. Both these ideas could easily have fitted into the 'transport' or 'experience' categories that I've (roughly) created in this book, but that's another thing about the sharing economy, it can be a bit messy. Like me. Maybe that's why I like it so much. And finally . . . ticket swapping: yes, that's right, actually exchanging your travel tickets themselves with somebody else. But is this sharing, or just trading? I thought I'd pop it in anyway, just in case you thought I'd forgotten.

So, there are a few different ways that the sharing economy can make travel more sustainable, more enjoyable, and easier. But what are the downsides? We've talked about the home sharing model and the problems that have come with the growth of that. Aside from this, it's worth taking into account that with the sharing economy, as I've mentioned before, you don't have either the same choice or the same availability that you might do normally. So when it comes to travel, which often means making sure you get what you want for a specific timeframe when, perhaps, you've booked time off work, or schools are on holiday – it's important to plan well in advance. And pay extra attention to those reviews and star ratings: holidays are precious, so it's even more important than usual that nothing goes wrong.

As for advantages, well, there are many, and it all depends on which type of sharing economy travel platform you are using. You can bask in that warm glow that comes with knowing you did your bit for the planet, you can find a bit of human connection that warms your heart (I'm talking to you, Ruth), or you can do something for a lot less cash than you anticipated. Or even earn some, if you can be the sharer in the equation, rather than the sharee. The sharing economy and travel are perfect bedfellows: we don't travel all the time, so our assets are often unused or under-used, whether that's a tent, a camper van, a room, a boat, or even just space in our suitcase.

―――

The burlexercise has in fact left me aching in all the right places, and by right I mean places that don't often ache, suggesting I don't use them enough. In retrospect, it was quite fun, especially the bit to *Lady Marmalade*, although I don't think anyone would want to *coucher avec moi ce soir* after seeing that. I leave a review for Natasha on the skill sharing site: 'Great class!' and then something about her being 'encouraging' and how I would 'recommend!' I wait for Natasha to say something about me, perhaps along the lines of that she can't believe I haven't done burlesque before, or that she's never seen anyone perform so elegantly with a vacuum cleaner in the background. Her review is slow to appear, and when it does, it simply says 'It was great to have Eleanor join us in class'. Right. So it was 'great' that I joined the class. And that's it? I think that's what my stepdaughter would call 'shade'.

My spirits lift as I notice while logged in that I have also had a 'request', for an hour of copywriting, from someone called Wren. This is very exciting as I have my eye on an offering from Hilary called 'Repotting House Plants', and if I do the copywriting then I will have an hour's credit to use. In our new place, I've got quite into house plants: it's a lot brighter than where we lived before, which in theory should improve survival rates. However, like most domestic activities that I undertake, it is proving to be a mixed bag success-wise, as I'm not particularly green-fingered. In fact, there has been some collateral house plant damage, and suffice to say I will not be buying a Hoya (for 'hard to maintain' read 'easy to kill'), a Nerve Plant (which got on mine, by not growing, ever) or a Money Plant (ironic as it cost 15 quid and then rotted) ever again. But I think with some repotting advice from an expert, I could turn things around.

But first I have to earn my hour. After a few messages, Wren and I firm up a time for me to spend an hour helping with her website, which I learn is for her own business: she is a pagan celebrant, specialising in weddings, funerals and 'rites of passage'. In fact it's the 'rites of passage' page of her site she wants help with, ironically (or coincidentally?), as this is a skill sharing rite of passage for me. However, I am unsure as to what other rites of passage there are, so decide before our session to investigate so I am not either surprised or confused when the time comes.

As it turns out, there are plenty of types of rites of passage that apparently require a celebrant. Some of these I get, like naming a baby, or adoption, or coming of age. Some of them I understand slightly less, maybe because of my own experiences: pregnancy, for one. The thought of having a celebrant hanging around when I was angrily waddling about with indigestion is nothing short of unfathomable. Moving home: also not really one that says 'let's meet in the woods and burn sage', more 'let's get on with the packing because the removal men will be here in an hour'. First blood: well, I've bookmarked a page on Google for when that happens to my daughter but it's less about celebrating, more about 'send me some of those fancy period pants everyone uses these days'.

But this is not about me, this is about sharing my skills, and helping Wren – and also of course earning my hour of credit so I can do something else, because I'm getting quite into this whole skill sharing thing. So I reserve judgement and take a deep breath, as I can see Wren spells magic 'Magick' and that suggests she might even push the limits of my woo-woo, which I would say are above average. We shall see: the sharing economy is all about new experiences, and I am nothing if not game.

Wren has sent me a Zoom link which I dutifully join at the allotted time of 2pm. I'm reading a news article (OK, Instagram) so I don't notice the minutes tick by until I spot it's already 2.05pm. I'm a patient woman but five minutes without explanation is heading towards rude. Then, Zoom flickers into life and I see Wren. She doesn't apologise, but instead looks at me with glittery eyes to the point where I wonder if she's slightly stoned. She's got a long mane of grey hair but what I notice before this is that she is wearing a huge necklace that appears to be in the shape of a vagina. Or, more accurately, a vulva. It's admirable, but also slightly disconcerting and as much as I try to focus on Wren, who I am now convinced is stoned, my eyes get drawn to her collarbone, which is not where you would normally expect to see a fairly large clitoris winking back at you like the erstwhile gaffer-taped wing mirror on Cumulo Mumbus. All I can think about is what the necklace is made of, and who made it. And why.

Wren is quite open-minded about the (fairly terrible) copy on her website, which is either because she is a 'lightworker' (or so she tells me), or because she is stoned. Or because she doesn't care. I can't work it out, and the hour limps by with me trying to form coherent sentences – that include the essential features and benefits – out of strings of words like 'threshold' and 'alchemy'. At about 2.45pm, which is only forty minutes into the allocated hour due to Wren being late, she starts yawning profusely, picks her nose, and then tells me she is feeling 'blocked' because Mercury is retrograde. Same, girl, same. And then she's gone, in a puff of mystical smoke (or was it actual smoke – I genuinely think when she turned her camera off intermittently it was to inhale on a bong). Anyway, forty minutes has earned me an hour of someone else's skill. And I say 'someone else's' emphatically, because I have spotted

Wren has a listing called 'Tending To Your Inner Fire', and I can say with absolute certainty that I won't be using my hour's credit on that.

———

I didn't realise, until I spoke again to Dr Matt Cole of the University of Birmingham's history department, that a place which played a part in the history of skill sharing was right on my doorstep. New Lanark, under an hour from Edinburgh, is a real village, but it's also a UNESCO World Heritage Site, because it was founded, in 1785, with a pioneering focus on shared resources, and the education and welfare of its mill worker residents. As a family, we've visited many times, and we call it 'Annie McLeod's House' – a name given to it by my stepdaughter Becca when she was little, Annie McLeod being the name of the mill worker girl whose story is told at the visitor's centre. And now the place has been made even more special for me, as I find out that Robert Owen, New Lanark's founder, helped shape the co-operative movement and, in a way, the sharing economy itself. On our visits, I've always been fascinated by what this philanthropist was trying to achieve – he seemed ahead of his time in many ways.

Matt tells me about Owen's attempts to develop 'labour notes' that enabled work to be exchanged without profit by business owners, and how he founded the National Equitable Labour Exchange in London in 1832. 'The idea was to create a currency based on work: in his own newspaper, which was called *The Crisis*, Owen said that "all wealth proceeded from labour and knowledge" and that time should be "the standard or measure of wealth". The labour notes he made, which were beautifully designed and looked just like bank notes, were based on hours, with an hour being worth sixpence. Goods were then exchanged for this new currency'.

For a while, it all went well, with plenty of traders agreeing to take the labour notes as payment. But problems arose – in the same way as they had for the ancient civilisations who bartered – around the value of what was being exchanged, and some people took advantage, meaning the value of the notes began to depreciate. As well as that, women were paid at a lower rate than men, which is unsurprising, considering it still happens now. The good news is that these women refused to sell their goods at the exchange unless they were offered equal terms; the bad news is that all of this, combined with some other issues concerning the property the exchange was housed in, meant the venture came to an end in 1834.

'Other similar projects to both this and New Lanark emerged, though,' Matt tells me, 'including Bournville in Birmingham and Port Sunlight in Merseyside, where an employer set out shared housing, educational and recreational facilities for their workers, and some shared work went on in these.' Something tells me Owen would have been pretty keen on the sharing economy, if he was alive today.

You had me at 'chloroform parties'

It was 1991, August, and a scorching summer in Oxford, as it always was, or at least, that's how I remember it. My obsession at the time was Guns N' Roses: Axl's trademark caterwauling and enviable range of bandanas had entranced me since 'Sweet Child O' Mine' came out a couple of years before, and I was finally off to see the band at Wembley for their Use Your Illusion tour (supported by Skid Row and Nine Inch Nails).

I wasn't really a bona fide rocker, I don't think I knew *what* I was to be honest, being a teenager, but I did know that I loved Axl and that there was every chance that if we met, he would love me too. So, with what I recall to be very little effort, I purchased a ticket for the gig from Our Price on Cornmarket Street, got change from £20 to cover the Oxford Tube to London, and enlisted a male friend-of-a-friend, who also liked the fabled GN'R, to come with me. It was part of the deal, to keep my mother happy, that I went with a boy to such a 'wild' event.

It was as hot, beer-soaked and rock 'n' roll as I could have imagined. Axl was wearing a kilt that was so long it looked more like a wraparound skirt, but I didn't care: he ran manically from one side of the stage to the other, throwing his mic stand about and wailing as only he knows how. Slash in the meantime was on guitar solo fire, face invisible under his trademark hair, cigarette resolutely in place for the duration of the concert. We got right down the front, on the left, just in time for the encore, which was 'Paradise City'. It was carnage: men were throwing beer, women were taking their tops off, and I was jostled from side to side, half thrilled at the chaos, half desperate not to lose my companion, because in the days before mobile phones, that would have been a disaster. But I didn't lose him, and drunk and sunburnt, we traipsed home to Oxford at the end of the night, safe in the knowledge that we'd just had one of the most memorable experiences of our lives.

That is how an experience should make you feel and surely, that is how easy it should be to have it? But this was thirty years ago, and times have changed. For one thing, tickets to see GN'R this summer (yes you can still see them, and marvel at the amount of work Axl has (ostensibly) had done to his once-perfect visage), will set you back hundreds. In fact for the 'Ultimate Package', the price goes into four figures, although I'm not sure what that includes . . . the chance to try on Axl's wraparound skirt? Now I get that, thanks to streaming services making music free to listen to in many cases, artists need to charge more for their live events, otherwise how else do they make money? But in the process, experiences like this have become expensive (some sites even now have 'surge pricing' that pushes ticket costs up even more when a concert is particularly popular), corporate and somehow less authentic than they used to be when they cost a single crisp banknote, including travel.

You might be wondering how the sharing economy can work its magic here. How do you borrow, rent or swap something as abstract as an 'experience'? And what are the benefits of doing so? The beauty of the sharing economy is that as well as allowing you to share things, and space, and skills – it also allows you to tap into experiences. In this experience economy, the focus is less on sustainable living, and more on community and the chance to access something you have never been able to before.

There are many different experiences you can 'share', but let's talk about music first. I was introduced a while back to Anne Dvinge, who founded a music experience sharing platform called Low-Fi, in Denmark. It is peer-to-peer, connecting individual musicians with hosts, who co-create mini concerts in their homes and other unique spaces. 'Live music first entered this space with booking platforms for live bands and music teachers. Strictly speaking, these types of platforms are based on a gig economy model, with sellers offering a service. Sharing economy models are less common and more complex, but marketplaces for live performances are gaining traction. These marketplaces build communities and infrastructure for artists, hosts and audiences to connect and co-create.'

I ask Anne what the benefits are of this. 'The sharing economy can provide greater democratisation to an industry by providing access,' she tells me. 'Marketplaces for live music, whether it's band booking, music lessons or concert co-creation are all part of a movement that sidesteps the usual gatekeeper in the music industry and enables better access for the ordinary consumer and more ways for artists and musicians to earn money. However, the type of platform where focus is on the community and the co-creation adds another layer of active music consumption: at these concerts, which are most often small house shows, every person in the room, the host, the artist and the audience are all active creators of the moment and responsible for the moment. This type of concert cannot, in the same way as a more traditional show in a professional venue, be pre-packaged and produced as there are simply too many variables that lie just slightly out of anyone's control. Every concert is a unique combination of the host, the artist and the audience.

'The home concert is of course not something new – actually it is probably the oldest format in existence, dating back to people making music together round the fire – although the concept of a "concert" is much later. Prior to recorded and radio transmitted music, this was how we created and listened to music. But also chamber music, the salon concert, rent parties, garage rock and basement/loft shows are all variations on this format. "House shows" exist and take place in almost every corner of the world. Into this comes platform technology, providing access and infrastructure – allowing people to connect and gather across immediate networks and social circles.'

––––

So this is music – what about other experiences in people's homes, accessed peer-to-peer? Also gaining popularity are sharing economy food experiences. What is being shared here is someone's home, their cooking skills, and indeed their food – and sometimes, it is also a shared experience with other guests. I have a date in my diary to go out with my friend Jude, who I haven't seen for ages, but as I am borrowing, renting and swapping, this can't be a 'normal' evening out – of course it will be a sharing economy one.

I register on a platform that specialises in exactly this: shared, 'at home' experiences. The following evening, Jude and I rideshare down to Leith, the docks area of Edinburgh which is a little edgier than our side of town but also has an impressive array of cool bars and restaurants. Which we aren't going to. No, instead, we head to a modern apartment block just beside the harbour, the address of which has been texted to me that day by the platform in question.

We have booked an 'at home dining experience' which is a Scottish-Italian tasting menu, of no less than eight courses. I long for my Amish dress with the overindulgence-friendly lacing at the front but instead have opted for what I think seems appropriate for sitting in someone else's living room: a low-key (and also rented) RIXO dress with a deliberately clashing mix of prints. Neither of us know what to expect: will there be other people there? Will it be weird being in a stranger's house? Will it matter that we are late? (Which we are, because we run into Malmaison to buy a bottle of wine as it's 'bring our own', but are rudely waylaid by two pints of Birra Moretti. OK, two each.).

We arrive at the door at the same time as a Deliveroo rider, prompting Jude and I to exchange glances which indicate that we both wonder how 'home-cooked' this food will turn out to be. However, the Deliveroo is for another apartment, and we are buzzed in by our host Federica, who welcomes us warmly. She is dressed in chef's whites but for a second the look is more dental surgery than gastronomical experience. I think it's because we're not in a restaurant, so it looks a bit out of context, but after a brief root canal flashback I move on from this and Federica shows us into her living room.

The lights are dim and in the corner of the room is a table set for two, while the rest of the room seems slightly bare. The place settings are restaurant style, beautiful folded linen napkins, wine glasses for red and white wine, and slate placemats. It all looks . . . lovely. But still slightly odd. Jude and I politely argue about who will sit where, and Federica disappears into the kitchen, which looks small and is directly off the living room.

Just as Jude and I are about to burst into nervous laughter, Federica reappears with our hastily purchased (and inappropriately French) wine, pours it, and starts telling us about the region of Italy she is from. Then she asks us both to look at the wall, which for a second is frankly terrifying, and I fear that I'm having my second brush with the Mafia (the first being when I worked in Sicily as an au pair between school and university, but that's another story). Then I notice that the wall has what appears to be a white sheet, possibly a duvet cover, loosely attached to it.

Federica switches on a projector which is perched on a nearby bookcase, and a short film about her particular region of Italy starts to play on the wall. I think the sheet/duvet cover is intended to act as a screen and make the experience more cinematic. But the problem is that at the angle I'm sitting, I can't see the film at all, just a crumpled sheet, accompanied by a slightly robotic American voice talking over some traditional music about paradise beaches, crystalline water and a myriad of something which I can't make out. Jude and I take huge slurps of the French wine.

Having just spent ten minutes looking at a duvet cover listening to Italian folk music, the canapés frankly can't come soon enough. Federica brings out some traditional homemade bread, which is more like tortilla chips, and an olive oil made by an unnamed relative. Alongside this are some interesting canapés, a mini bruschetta, a kind of spicy rice ball and some sort of squid thing, which she talks through enthusiastically, explaining the locally sourced ingredients and the Italian recipe behind them. It's all delicious, and Jude and I feel more at ease now, thanks to the wine, which has also given me the confidence to speak Italian a bit to Federica, who seems delighted and from then on switches between both languages.

Course after course arrives at the table: pasta with basil, a smoked haddock risotto, aubergines with salmon, sea bass hidden under courgettes. Federica opens the bottle of Italian red we have pre-ordered as part of the meal, and it is strong – what I imagine Adrian the wine expert would describe as 'complex'. With each dish we gulp more of it and chat as two people who haven't seen each other for a while do. As course six arrives, Jude leans over the table and says, 'Is it just me or do you feel really pissed?' I do Jude, I do, but to be honest, course after course of home-made food, and speaking slurred but not-too-shabby Italian, in turn with chatting to a good friend is all making it a very happy pissed.

We push through to course seven, thankfully a palate-cleansing sorbet with thyme (delicious), and then course eight arrives, which is a chocolate and espresso panna cotta, as wobbly and unctuous as any panna cotta should be. I stop short of licking the plate. Then Federica brings out a local digestif which is a liqueur made of myrtle, and after a very unsuccessful attempt to discuss, in Italian, the Greek myth of Aphrodite and her connection to this plant, which seems to have translated into Jude's grandmother being called Myrtle, we realise it's time to go. We roll into another rideshare and head back to the Southside, discussing whether we had a look through Federica's skincare products when we were in her bathroom. I did, Jude didn't.

———

To find out a bit more about shared food experiences, I ask Laura Arciniegas who is a sociology researcher working at EatWith, a platform that connects hosts who want to cook in their home with people who would like to share a meal with them. She says:

'Traditionally, we gather around food with family and friends, using it as a vehicle to create and maintain social bonds. What the collaborative economy and technological advances have done is given this possibility to people who don't know each other. Of course at the same time it allows talented cooks who are passionate about what they do (and don't have a restaurant) the opportunity to showcase their skills.

'Modern times are characterised by the feeling that the world is becoming more and more "anonymous"; the same has happened with food. The sharing economy allows us to connect with what is genuine, creating authentic feelings through a real person (the host), and real social connections (the other guests), as opposed to a restaurant which could be seen as an impersonal place.

'The "commensal table" is a reciprocal space where social and cultural differences exist and political views and values are expressed, and therefore it's the perfect place for both discussion and connecting with the world. The concept is age-old: think of a Mediterranean table where people gather for hours to eat, or a wedding where food is served to celebrate, or family dinners on Sundays. Platforms like this are both a revival and a modern response: they combine a mix of those very familiar and intimate situations with the restaurant idea of strangers eating together at the same time.'

Jude and I didn't discuss politics, as far as I can remember, but we certainly 'gathered for hours to eat' and had an experience that was completely different to going to a 'normal' restaurant. It felt personal, it felt real – it felt like we made a connection with another culture, with Federica, and with each other. Peer-to-peer doesn't have to just be about a 'thing', and actually when it's about something as intangible as an experience, it seems like the sharing economy is more powerful than ever.

————

I have an hour of time in my skill sharing 'time bank' from the copywriting with Wren, so I decide to cash it in. I'm quite tempted by an hour of chess, as Jake has been playing it a fair bit recently – although he only recently stopped calling it 'chest', so I'm wondering exactly how good he really is. Still, it would be something for us to do together, in the absence of my inability to kill renegade robots. There's also a Pensions Q&A (too depressing), Thrifty Cooking (which as we know I can do – or think I can – already) and a Body Confidence Kickstart, which after burlesque-gate might be a wise idea. However, I plump for my original plan of

Hilary's Repotting House Plants, and book her in for the following week.

Hilary sends me a few messages prior to our virtual meeting asking me if I have potting compost, and 'a range of pot sizes', as well as 'broken crockery'. I do actually have some of these things, and although it is all outside the back door and covered in slugs, I consider this a triumph. Shortly before our Zoom, I spread newspaper over the kitchen table, grab all of my houseplants that look like they need help and bring my slug-covered pots inside. I feel like a skill sharing pro, especially as the hour for this session was honestly earned, albeit by forty minutes of watching someone smoke weed and pick their nose. Hilary, in contrast to Wren, is a smiley, earthy delight, genuinely interested in houseplants and their many woes, and clearly a lot more experienced in indoor horticulture than me.

The hour flies by as I show her plant after plant and she advises on whether I should 'pot up', 'pot down' (this is a thing, which I didn't know about), or do something else like move the plant to a shadier spot or water less/more. I also find out you don't always need to put stones or broken crockery at the bottom of pots. I often try to get this level of advice by hanging about the cash desk at the local plant shop, but when you do that you've really only got until the next customer comes along. In the final ten minutes, I show her Jonathan, the only plant I own which has a name. It is – or should I say they are – a Calathea that my sister gave me, a highly temperamental and at times rather over-dramatic plant which Phoebe and I named after Jonathan Van Ness from *Queer Eye*. But in spite of being high-maintenance, and preferring to be misted daily, it is a joy to behold, a bouquet of huge, tiger-striped oval leaves, the patterns appearing to have been painted on by a Post-Impressionist. At night, these leaves lift up to reveal purple undersides, and then open out again during the day, as if saluting the sun. I love it.

Controversially, Hilary suggests that Jonathan needs to be divided, which is how you propagate this type of plant. I am concerned about how Jonathan will react to this, and I am no less concerned about what we will call the resulting Jonathans. After my call with Hilary, which, incidentally, I rate five stars on the skill sharing website, Phoebe returns from school and we discuss – at length – the naming issue, deciding that the end goal here would be, obviously, to have many Calatheas, each named after a member of the Fab Five. It's an unusual end goal, but one I am willing to work towards.

————

The relationship you have with your sibling is usually the longest relationship of your life. So I am grateful (not in an Instagram hashtag way) that my sister and I are good friends and we make time to see each other every couple of weeks – sometimes with our respective children, other times just the two of us, so that we can chat as only two people who grew up together can. Usually, this involves a simple coffee at a nearby café, which is quite often exactly what we need. But it is also just that: coffee and a chat. So, when my sister – who is a doctor, and works a lot harder than me in a hospital doing serious, admirable stuff – messages me to arrange one of our regular meetups, I decide, as part of my exploration of the sharing economy, to suggest instead that we have an 'experience'. This experience is restricted in the sense that it needs to be on a Wednesday morning (due to my sister's working hours), and in Edinburgh, and has to be booked via an experience sharing platform. This should be easy then.

I sign up with one of the many peer-to-peer platforms that offer tours and experiences led by locals, which have flourished in recent years – although they obviously, like a lot of travel-related sharing economy platforms, took a hit during the pandemic. The tours and experiences are led by locals who list themselves, or share themselves, in a similar way to skill sharing on a platform. Their skill, however, is that they live in the place in question, and have 'insider' knowledge, and that's what they share with you. These 'nonprofessional' tour guides are bringing back a more – and I wince a bit when I resort to this overused adjective again, but you know what I mean – *authentic* experience: one that's a world away from the corporate tours we're all used to. If you have ever followed a yellow umbrella around a city, while a script is shouted at you by someone who is clearly as local as you are – consider this the antidote.

The challenge here is that we are locals, albeit expats – but we *have* been in Edinburgh long enough to know all the usual stories from the Southside: that it's good luck to spit on the Heart of Midlothian on the Royal Mile – I tend to cross over just so I don't have to see all the little bubbling pools of saliva; the story of Greyfriars Bobby – where I take Marley for a walk: the whole loyal dog/sit on your master's grave thing is apparently not true anyway; the One O'clock Gun – the cannon fired from the castle every day at 1pm, for sailors to set their clocks by in the Firth of Forth (it still makes you jump if you're walking through the Grassmarket at that time, no matter how long you've lived here).

We know these – we live here. What I am looking for is emphatically not this kind of thing. But what could it be? Something which really opens our eyes to what is right under our noses, something that piques our interest, something that leaves us feeling entertained and illuminated? And then I see it: a 'Marvellous Medical Tour' of the Southside, courtesy of a local guide called Euan. It promises 'unbelievable true stories; from grave robbers, to the real-life Sherlock Holmes, surgeries gone wrong, plague doctors, suffragettes, chloroform parties, eighteenth century sexologists and much, much more . . .'. Euan, I'll stop you now, you had me at 'chloroform parties'. I book it, for the price of our usual brace of coffees and scones, and we arrange to meet Euan the following Wednesday.

———

Skill sharing, unsurprisingly, seems to have its own set of pros and cons. Before we get onto them, let's talk briefly about the difference between skill sharing and the other way that services can be accessed on apps and platforms. Sitting alongside the sharing economy are a growing number of platforms that allow people to share a skill for money – anything from childcare to handyman services, right through to graphic design or business consulting. These skills are bought, not 'swapped' for others, so I haven't included this way of doing things in these pages.

Definitions are always up for debate, but many people call these 'gig platforms' – the 'gig' being the piece of work. The term 'gig economy' has, however, come to be associated specifically with the kind of gig work that rideshare and delivery drivers do, and because of this has gained a bad reputation for low wages and a lack of employment rights. I think that gig work or platform work should really mean any ad-hoc work that is accessed through an online platform or app, but that's just my opinion, and I know that not everyone would agree.

Back to the skill sharing I've been doing, and I'll start with the pros. You get people's expertise without having to pay for it – well, you *do* have to pay for it, just in a different way. What skill sharing allows you to do is exchange something you find easy with something you find hard, or can't do at all, so it seems really logical and seamless. You also feel as though you're genuinely doing someone a favour when you skill share with them, even though you're getting a credit for it. And when you're on the receiving end, it feels like you're getting something – like Hilary's plant advice – for free. It's quite heavy on the warm glow in that respect, in spite of there not being as many of the more obvious sharing economy benefits this time round, like reducing your carbon footprint. But some types of sharing are good for communities: the skills you need are probably out there, locally, and this allows you to tap into them, make connections and save money. It's like Robert Owen's vision has been waiting to be brought back to life, and now that the technology is ready, we can do just that.

Another positive aspect of skill sharing is that it allows you to try out new things. I would never have done any of the things I did by hiring someone and yet I got a professional wine expert, a personal trainer and a plant guru at my disposal for an entire hour each. The flip side of this is that if you want to get started with a passion project, you could use a sharing platform to share your new skill, try it out and see if people enjoy it. And not just try new things either – skill sharing could revive long lost talents: I love the idea of a platform like this helping the older generation pass on skills to younger people. Imagine being able to get an hour of knitting instruction from pros like my mother or mother-in-law? To a Millennial crafter, that would be worth its weight in wool.

So what are the negatives? Deciding what skill I would share and listing it on my profile was probably the fiddliest part but it really didn't take that long, and I got booked fairly quickly. If you're busy with paid work, you could feel as though you don't have time, but it is only an hour here and there to build up some credit. Then there are the skills that you can choose from, which vary from platform to platform. On some you can find things like yoga, on others much more practical skills such as bookkeeping that could help you, or your small business if you have one. So I suppose you need to be conscious that you might not find exactly what you're looking for, but as these communities grow, you are more likely to find skills you need, and so will other people. It's the same as any sharing platform: the more of us that do it, the better it will be for everyone.

I take Adrian's advice and when I have enough money, I start buying an extra bottle of wine, and amazingly enough – not drinking it, but putting it in the cupboard on a new wine rack that I got on the 'non-food' section of the food sharing app. It's not particularly stylish but who cares, I have wine that is not currently open, and I feel like a grown-up. As for burlesque, I think it's safe to say Dita Von Teese won't be asking me to support her on tour any time soon but it was fun, and my glutes thanked me the next day. But one of the happiest outcomes of skill sharing is the fact that in the kitchen, lifting purple leaves up and down in time with the rising and setting sun, is now not just Jonathan, our 'OG' Calathea, but Tan and Karamo too.

———

My sister and I meet Euan at Greyfriars Bobby, which is where he suggests (I nearly ask him to change it because I feel this book has too many mentions of said dog). But meet Euan we do near the fabled statue at 9am, which to me is early – to my sister, probably not so much. Euan is young, in his early twenties I think, with an earnest face and a haircut that your grandmother would approve of. I realise immediately that there won't be anyone else on the tour, just me and my sister, who is eyeing me in a 'What the hell is this?' type way last used when I introduced her to my boyfriend Gary in 1992. It feels slightly awkward to begin with, but it's a beautiful spring day so we all talk manically for the first few minutes about the weather while Euan leads us into Greyfriars Kirkyard to start the tour.

Thankfully, it's not about the dog, (or should I say dogs – the whole Greyfriars Bobby thing was revealed quite recently to have been a Victorian publicity stunt involving not one but two dogs – and this is categorically my last mention of the 'legend' in this book, or ever.) What Euan is showing us is in fact something I have seen when walking Marley, and been curious about: a kind of metal cage over one of the old gravestones, which he tells us is a 'mortsafe', used to stop people stealing bodies for dissection. They only had to use the cages until the bodies decomposed, apparently, because after that corpses were of no use to the anatomists. So we're right in at the deep end then, Euan? I start to regret my hastily eaten peach yoghurt with coffee chaser, and mull over intermittent fasting as a life choice, mainly to block out Euan saying words like 'cadaver' and 'exhume'. I glance at my sister who is engrossed, telling Euan about her cadaver that she shared with other students at medical school. I won't be doing a chapter on that, I can assure you.

We wander around the university area, from the medical school where Euan tells us why people from the UK are known abroad as 'Limeys' (British sailors were called this because they were given limes to prevent scurvy) to cobbled George Square, where he shares a story about the inspiration for Sherlock Holmes. We stop by the Meadows, the Surgeons Hall, all the while stepping in and out of warm sunshine and cooler, dappled tree shade, and chattering away to Euan, who knows way more than just his tour facts.

At Potterrow he tells us the tale of James Graham, a Georgian 'sexologist' who learned about electricity in America, then returned to the UK to set up the Temple of Health in London, which was most famous for its Grand State Celestial Bed, a kind of marital aid which featured live turtle doves, electro magnetics, flowers and even therapeutic 'gases'. Euan points down to Buccleuch Street, where Graham died, and where my sister lived as a student. It's so interesting that the slightly uncomfortable feeling of having a man twenty years younger than us talk about 'marital aids' suddenly doesn't matter.

Instead of being in a rush to get to wherever, we have looked up at the buildings we walk past every day, and listened to their stories. We have heard them tell us they weren't always just homes for people like us, but for storytellers, suffragettes, murderers, scientists . . . It makes sense: Edinburgh has always been more than the sum of its parts, more than turrets and cobblestones, and the haar, that sea mist which sits over the city so stubbornly when it feels like the rest of the country is basking in the sun. No, it is more than that, more than its physical form, it is all the Burgh people who came before, and will come after.

———

Who is the Euan of the past that technology has reconnected us with? I ask historian Dr Amy Miller, author of *The Globetrotter: Victorian Excursions in India, China and Japan*.

'In the Victorian era, local guides were used in conjunction with the travellers' handbooks and in fact, advertised their services in these. They were part of a desire to be seen as a traveller rather than a tourist. That meant that you engaged with local populations and experiences that represented the 'authentic' rather than merely a superfluous cultural experience. The guides were an important part of accessing what was believed to be authentic.

'In Britain, there were two major trends in the late eighteenth century that are tied to accessing both the practical knowledge that a local guide had as well as that local knowledge that was tied to a sense of place. The first was a touristic interest in the Lake District: this was fuelled by the work of Wordsworth and an emphasis on the landscape. The second is the Grand Tour – a trip of Europe, typically undertaken by young men, which began in the seventeenth century and went through to the mid-nineteenth. During the tour, a *cicerone* would be hired, who had what many tourists saw as a beguiling combination of an almost folkloric knowledge of Rome, the campagna and specifically the forum paired with a very good working knowledge of history and archaeology. There were families that had generations of *cicerones* that were considered the top guides.

'The local guides were integral to creating a sense of place,' Amy continues. This certainly resonates with what we experienced from Euan. 'In some cases that was about immersing yourself in a particular landscape, or cityscape. They also played a key role in shopping and helping travellers to find those objects that would become the material representation of their journey and experiences. Guides were key to interpreting the site and telling people what to observe and even how to feel.'

So what happened in the early days of tourism sets the scene for this tech-powered access to local guides that I'm trying now a century and a half later: a realisation that to get to know a place, the best person to talk to is someone who cares about it – not just someone who can show you a checklist of landmarks.

———

Experiences can have ripples that last a lifetime: that Guns N' Roses gig did. I shared it, unbeknown to me at the time, with my future husband. I wouldn't meet him for another decade, but he was there at Wembley that day too, also down at the front on the left, and probably less bothered about being jostled than I was. Maybe we jostled each other, who knows?

Years later, when Jake was born, we did that thing new parents do with their first, and googled to see who he shared a birthday with. Woody Harrelson, Daniel Radcliffe . . . and there it was: Slash. How appropriate, considering the first time his parents' paths had crossed. Then, when Phoebe came along, we did the same, although probably not for a while, you know how it is with the second baby. She shares her birthday with Zsa Zsa Gabor, Ronald Raegan . . . and Axl Rose.

As for my sister and I, we will still drink coffee and talk about our families – this is what siblings do. But after our walk with Euan, I feel like we're no longer limited by whether to get a scone or a croissant: we decide to do 'more of this sort of thing'. On a different platform, there's some 'Forest Bathing'. I'm no Wren, but as I mentioned, I'm a little bit woo-woo, and more so than my down-to-earth doctor sister (no criticism, we need down-to-earth people like her). I wonder if she'd go for that? Or maybe 'Tea with A Naughty Sheep'? This promises both a 'special feeling' and a chance to 'enter the secret world of sheep'. I've entered a lot of secret worlds recently, thanks to this experiment: Use By date forgery, fashion photography, canine communication and chloroform parties . . . which I realise I didn't tell you about. They were parties where people tested out different types of anaesthesia. I'm going to pass. (Not pass out.)

Anyway, whether or not we go on to bathe in a forest, we did something pretty cool that day, as did Jude and I when we went to Federica's for dinner. A sharing economy experience, but also a shared experience. So what have I learnt about experience sharing? First of all, you're not always going to find what you set out to – you have to keep an open mind – but in a way, that's a pro rather than a con. Another pro is that by using an experience sharing platform you get access to things you wouldn't normally.

As well as this, you get the pleasant feeling (again) that you're doing something not just differently, but more positively. Admittedly, it hasn't got that clear environmental benefit, but I did warn you about that at the start. What else? The people I've dealt with have all been very friendly, and I can see that if you used platforms like this regularly enough, particularly the 'eat in people's homes' ones, you would certainly feel part of a community.

I'm sold on experience sharing. I think as we get older, we 'do' less things with our friends and have fewer experiences with them. Sure, we meet up, we have a coffee, a meal, a drink. But what about doing things, rather than just reminiscing about when we *used* to do things? Having experiences that we'll remember in ten or twenty years? Because I'm not sure we'll look back and say, 'Remember that scone you had in 2022?' We can still do things that are worth talking about: we can bathe in a forest, tell off that naughty sheep (if that's the 'done thing'), or even just make sushi, or taste gin, or . . . The sharing economy isn't the only way to do it, but it's one way. And then our memories of each other's company won't just be a conversation over the top of two flat whites.

A guide to sharing – part two

What are the benefits?

- Car owners can make money when their car would otherwise be sitting idle, while those without a car, or the need for an extra vehicle, can access one cheaply and locally.
- Car sharing reduces the number of stationary cars, which cuts parking times and makes cities more efficient.
- Fewer people will buy new cars (or second cars) if they car share and more people will try electric vehicles.
- Other types of transport sharing (bike/van/others) also mean one less item manufactured, which is better for the planet.

Do...

Make sure you have an up-to-date driving licence and ID ready when you want to sign up.

Leave time at the beginning and end of your rental period to take photos of the car.

If you're renting out your car or bike, take time with the description and pricing so it's appealing to renters.

Don't...

Expect your car to get rented out immediately, especially if there aren't many users in your area.

Return the car or bike you rented in anything other than the same condition you got it in.

Forget to tell your friends about it – the more the merrier.

What to use

In the UK/Europe	In the US/Canada	In Australia
Hiyacar	Communauto	Car Next Door
Karshare	RideAlike	GoGet
Liftshare	Turo	Zipcar
Getaround	Getaround	Flexicar
Enterprise Car Club	Maven	Popcar
Turo	HyreCar	
Ubeeqo	Zipcar	**Bikes** (most operate globally)
Zipcar	Enterprise	Spinlister
MyWheels	GIG	Cycle.land
Greenwheels	Riders-share.com (motorbikes)	Santander Cycles
SnappCar		HumanForest
BlaBlaCar		Swapfiets
CoCharger (electric vehicle charging share)		Dott
		Citi Bike
Borroad		Bikesharing schemes in many cities run by Lime, Lyft and others.

SPACE SHARING

What are the benefits?

- You can access space nearby and use it for a variety of purposes – for free or for less than more formal rentals.
- If you have space, you can rent it out to other people locally and make money.
- Many types of space sharing come with environmental benefits, others improve infrastructure and empower communities.
- Space sharing opens up possibilities and can give you access to experiences that you might not otherwise have had.

Do...

Share your space, if you have it, on a range of different platforms to improve the chances of someone requesting it and to support multiple sharing businesses.

Reserve spaces in advance as fewer options mean that they can get booked up fast.

Keep your options open: you might not find a parking, storage or work space exactly where you need it.

Don't...

Feel you have to order lots of food or drinks if you're using a shared workspace.

Expect to get requests to use your space immediately, this type of sharing takes time.

Use a space you're renting for anything other than what you've requested it for.

What to use

In the UK	In the US/Canada	In Australia
Park share:	Park share:	Spacer
Kerb, JustPark,	ParkStash,	Parkable
YourParkingSpace,	Neighbor,	Sharedspace
easyParking,	WhereiPark,	Rubberdesk
Park On My Drive,	SpotHero	Spacenow
Mobypark	Longer term	
Longer term	storage: Neighbor	
storage: Stashbee,	Creative spaces:	
Storemates	Splacer, Peerspace	
Creative spaces:	Gardens:	
mushRoom, Tutti	SharedEarth,	
Gardens: AllotMe,	Campspace	
Borrow my Garden,	Swimming pools:	
Campspace	Swimply	
Work space: Swurf,	Work space:	
Jarvo, Seats2meet	LiquidSpace,	
	Breather	

TRAVEL AND HOME SHARING

What are the benefits?

- Depending on the type of travel or home sharing you do, you are contributing to a more sustainable tourism industry.
- Home sharing allows people to travel (or live) more cheaply, and for homeowners it can provide support and company as well as an income.

- Travelling using the sharing economy can open up new experiences, more cheaply, than using big holiday companies.
- You get the chance to be part of a local community rather than just see the usual sights at a tourist destination.

Do...

Factor in time to get your home ready for swapping or sharing, and take good photos.

Leave reviews – trust is extra important when you're staying in someone's home.

Book early, especially if you're borrowing a tent or camper van in holiday season.

Don't...

Treat the homeshare that you're staying in like a hotel – it's someone's home.

Expect a five-star service, but do be friendly and courteous to your host or guests.

Forget that if you're carrying a parcel for someone to make sure the platform is legitimate and any customs clearance or duty payment obligations are being met.

What to use

Most home share platforms operate globally	HomeAway	Love Home Swap
	Wimdu	Teacher Home Swap
	Intervac	Workaway
Airbnb	CouchSurfing	Trustroots
Homestay	People Like Us	Behomm
FlipKey	HouseSit Match	HomeExchange.com

Nestful	**Other travel**	Camplify
BedyCasa	**related sharing**	Camptoo
Culture Go Go	**platforms**	Goboony
WWOOF	HolidaySwap	Yescapa
Homestayin	Worldpackers	CamperVanGuy.com
misterb&b	FundMyTravel	Escape
	Boatsetter	Campervans
Homeshare	Beds on Board	ReserveAmerica
sites for shared	Boataffair	RVezy
permanent living	GetMyBoat	RVshare
HomeshareUK.org	SamBoat	Outdoorsy
Homeshare Living	Click&Boat	Rent My Campa
Share and Care	Barqo	Indie Campers
Share My Home	Tentshare	
CareRooms	Hipcamp	

SKILL SHARING

What are the benefits?

- Skill sharing can save money for individuals as well as small businesses.
- You can use it to try out a new skill that you're learning, like yoga teaching or face painting, to build up your confidence and get feedback and reviews.
- Skill sharing allows you to try new things without any financial outlay.
- It encourages local connections and interactions with other people from different generations, cultures or backgrounds.

Do...

Give your profile, and what skills you will share, some thought, and try to list more than one.

Leave reviews as soon as you can to build trust in the skill sharing community.

Manage your expectations: you only get an hour of someone's time.

Don't...

Register unless you're willing to reciprocate skill sharing – it's a two-way street.

Assume you will get booked immediately; it can take time.

Forget to share what you're doing on social media if you can – the more people sign up, the more choice of skills there will be.

What to use

Most skill and work-related sharing platforms operate globally		
Timebanking.org	Fair Shares	TheHIVE
Economy of hours (ECHO)	Nomads Skillshare	My Language Exchange
Kesero	Roleshare (job share)	TimeRepublik
	AnyGood? (recommendation sharing)	Simbi
		HaveNeed

EXPERIENCE SHARING

What are the benefits?

- You can enjoy a peer-to-peer experience, whether that's music, food or tourism related.
- If you have a talent, you can use an experience platform to share that with the world.
- Shared experiences are more authentic, personal and less corporate, taking us back to the original ethos of whatever it is we're doing.
- Experience sharing is often cheaper than booking similar events using the usual methods.

Do...

Make sure you research thoroughly – new experience platforms are popping up all the time.

Leave reviews: individuals on these platforms rely on them to get more bookings.

Keep an open mind: some experiences are unusual, but nothing ventured . . .

Don't...

Expect to see the usual kind of concerts and restaurants, this is experience sharing and not the same.

Be late for any bookings if you can help it, you might be the only person coming.

Cancel at short notice: these events often take lots of advance preparation.

What to use

Most experience sharing platforms operate globally		
EatWith	ToursByLocals	Yoomers
Airbnb	GetYourGuide	Universe
Experiences	TravelLocal	Traveling Spoon
Sofar Sounds	TripUniq	BonAppetour
	Withlocals	Live At Yours
	Low-Fi	Music Collective

It's not over yet

So it's been a year, give or take a few weeks. Edinburgh has gone full circle with the seasons, from a Gothic short story, where it's practically dark at school pick-up and the smell of the brewery mixes with the fog – back to a smiling, leafy adventure, buzzing with festivals. And during that time, I've done my best to share, rent and swap as many of the things as possible that I would normally buy.

I've tried to be a guinea pig on your behalf, and pick out as many of the highlights – and lowlights – as I can. My family has helped me make up my mind about some of them too. And the ones I haven't attempted, I've told you about, at least as many as I can – it's never an exhaustive list as new sharing economy ideas pop up all the time. So what are we still doing, what did we only try once . . . and what was the best of the bunch?

Before we get on to that, let's talk about the sharing economy in general. It isn't *the* solution to our problems – if there was only one solution to our problems, that would be great, but unlikely. However, it could be *one* solution. As I read online recently, and I'm sorry that I don't remember where (maybe Instagram, my valued news source): 'We don't have to do everything, but we do have to do something.' It's true.

To (roughly) quote Jon Squire and Ian Brown of The Stone Roses: we stand on shifting sands. As I write this, the radio in the background is telling me about the temperature in London hitting 40° this weekend. It's the first national emergency of this sort that's been declared, and it's not a 'fun' ice cream eating situation, it's a red alert. It's the hottest period for 125,000 years[14] and we've only got two-and-a-half years left before emissions must peak to limit global temperature rises to 1.5°C. If you have to go and hang out in the chilled section of Waitrose just to cool down – in EDINBURGH – something is amiss. Very amiss. And by the way, polar bears *can* swim, faster than humans actually – but I now know that's not the point.

The point is, when it comes to the planet, if you've been putting off caring, sorry, but you can't anymore. I should know, I've been putting it off for ages. It's become an emergency, and in doing so, it's become personal – about you and me, not just other people who are more organised than us, or more 'green', or more 'into that sort of thing'. But I'm not here to tell you what to do, I'm here to tell you, here's one 'something' you can do. Because we all need to do something.

What I like most about the sharing economy, and you may have got this from reading the book, is that it can help

---

14 https://www.ipcc.ch/

the planet (I say 'can' because it doesn't *always*), but it also comes with a plethora of other benefits. It can help us save – and make – money, which is most welcome in a time of rising costs and inflation. It can help us to experience new things: also welcome after the collective trauma of the pandemic. And it can help us to connect with both local and online communities, supporting and empowering each other rather than big businesses, some of which are doing their utmost not to even pay their taxes.

Sharing with people around us, whether it's our homes, our space, our skills or our things, can also help us have a sense of purpose, make us feel less isolated or lonely, and support us to find friendships with people outside our usual 'tribes'. In other words, it can take us back to how we used to do things. And we can use technology to get to the best bits.

It makes so much sense, on so many levels, you'd think it would just be the way we do things, not something that's so special it needs a book written about it. It should just be 'the economy', not the sharing economy. Maybe one day, it will. It's certainly catching on – the total value of the global sharing economy is predicted to increase to around 335 billion US dollars by 2025, from only 15 billion US dollars in 2014.[15] I know this is business talk, but that's a big increase, and it shows that this peer-to-peer way of doing things is catching on (again).

There's another reason that the sharing economy is growing fast, and it's not just about the mess we're making of the planet. During the pandemic, many traditional

---

15 https://www.statista.com/statistics/830986/value-of-the-global-sharing-economy/

companies were forced to try new things – their survival depended on it. They had to move out of their comfort zones, perhaps by creating an entire staff of remote workers, or by suddenly having to use a platform to deliver goods that had previously been bought in person in a shop. People had to adapt – and quickly. And suddenly we were all online, using technology where we hadn't used before, reaching out locally because we couldn't travel, or trying to save or make money because we were furloughed. It wasn't a situation that any of us wanted, but it created an environment where certain types of sharing economy businesses could help us out – and, in turn, thrive themselves.

While we're talking business, one more thing – I said at the beginning that this isn't a business book, but I do want to talk a little about businesses and the sharing economy. Because so far, we have been considering what 'assets' we have as individuals that are under-used or not used at all. What happens if we apply that model to businesses, any businesses – tech, healthcare, education, transport – organisations with many departments or complex structures, or even smaller businesses who are part of networks, or share premises at retail or industrial parks. You get the picture: within these systems, there is a huge number of assets being used, but also being unused, or under-used. It could be anything, from medical equipment, to office furniture, to storage space. And if businesses shared, as well as individuals, it could be better for them financially, and a lot less wasteful.

The sharing economy for businesses is getting started, slowly. Lieke van Kerkhoven, founder of FLOOW2, a Netherlands-based company which helps businesses to share, tells me that for businesses, 'the sharing economy gives us the chance to move away from the destructive take-make-waste approach that has dominated our global economy for centuries. Like the circular economy, the model is based on nature: resources are endlessly used in cycles, and everything is interconnected. In such a system waste simply doesn't exist and resources and energy are kept within systems. But although technologically our species is ready for a new paradigm, such as the sharing economy, our mindset is still stuck in the industrial era. And this is reflected in the way we structure organisations, evaluate success, define value and hold on to a fiercely competitive culture.'

Back to what I've been up to. It's pretty obvious which bits I liked the most were, but let's recap. Food sharing certainly shone a light on how much we waste as a family, and I've made some positive changes in that respect, although please don't look in my salad drawers if you come round. I will certainly give away food again on the app and we still get Magic Bags regularly – that's one of my favourite new discoveries, and the kids love it too. I think it's a great mix of environmental feel-good, surprise and money-saving: like a sharing economy holy trinity. Through the Magic Bags, we've discovered new cafés and restaurants nearby that we've also gone to as 'normal' customers, and I've noticed more businesses joining that app, as well as another similar one starting up in Edinburgh.

Clothes sharing is a lot of fun, and I can't recommend it enough if you are sartorially challenged like me – or even if you're not. It has truly opened up a whole new world:

I no longer feel restricted by what I can afford to buy, or intimidated by expensive fashion shopping. In fact, it almost feels too enjoyable to be doing any good. And yet it is. During the time I've been using these apps, Phoebe has got heavily into 'thrifting', ie looking around charity shops for clothes, and other bits and bobs: I think it's a Gen Z trend. We go round these shops together, and I'm proud to say that my wardrobe (give or take a couple of Zara items from before my experiment began) is now a planet-friendly mix of shared clothes and second-hand.

We haven't got a dog – yet. We might one day, but in the meantime, there's a dog out there that not only knows who I am, but doesn't mind being in a photo with me. I've also stopped trying to make small talk with him. I'm not sure, but I think that might make me a Dog Person. I've still got some rented furniture, which we're still trying not to ruin, and if we need a one-off item like a carpet cleaner or a tent again, I'll definitely search on a sharing platform before I look elsewhere – but I'll probably double-check the map first. What else? I loved home sharing with Ruth in London, and will stay there again if Aunt Virginia's blow-up bed isn't available. I've used the park share app on a few occasions, and next time Cumulo Mumbus is in the garage, I've got my eye on that Vauxhall Corsa, because this time I might remember where it's parked.

As for skill sharing, this is definitely one of my favourites, and I'd love everyone who reads this book to get into it (especially if you're a plumber who specialises in toilet flushing), so we can all help each other and learn how to do new things. And finally, I'm going to ask my sister if she'll come and throw a pot with me instead of having a coffee next week (as in, on a potter's wheel, not just throw a pot). It was that or a 'Mindful Volcano Adventure' on Arthur's Seat, but I go there a lot these days anyway, ON MY BIKE. Take a moment to let that sink in. Yes, I bought a bike. And I'm not just using it for bike rides with my husband, but also for travel, instead of, sometimes, a car or taxi. You might wonder if the sharing economy is really meant to make people buy things, but what it did in this case was show me a better way.

Recently, I've noticed Jake saying something to me, other than 'When's dinner?' He sometimes asks, 'Is this ours?' about a random thing. It's like he gets now that not everything *is* ours. But it doesn't bother him, whether 'this' is a piece of furniture or an electronic item. I imagine he's just assessing how much damage he can do. This is disownership in action – a young, porous mind asking, but not caring. Why does it matter really, he thinks (or doesn't): it's here, I can use it, it's doing the job – whether we actually possess it or not just isn't the point. Gen Zs might just save us all – but in the meantime, I'm not going to sit here and let them take all the glory. Are you?

———

The other day, Phoebe and I went to walk Marley. We picked up a Magic Bag on the way so we could eat pastries in Greyfriars Kirkyard, on our favourite bench. When we got to Marjorie's, Marley trotted out to greet us, and threw himself on his back next to the Jack Russell themed front door mat, hoping for that belly tickle. And d'you know what? This time, I obliged.

Acknowledgements

Top of the list is my husband, as he is referred to in these pages – but he actually has a name: Andy. He's the person who I am happiest next to, and was a constant source of encouragement and support while I was writing *Thanks for Sharing* (and long before, for that matter). He also saved my life once, but that's another story. Thank you darling, you're bloody brilliant and I love you.

Jake and Phoebe: I know I'm biased, but you are both very, very cool humans. Thank you Jake for your endless hugs and your adorable randomness – you give teenagers a good name. And thank you Phoebe for being my constant companion and helper – you make everything more fun. And Becca, my excellent stepdaughter, you are always so supportive of your 'smum', and it is very much appreciated. We should do a duet sometime.

Thank you also to the rest of my wonderful family, who all rallied round with their stories, experiences and encouragement: my sister Ros, sister-in-law Laura, my mother Di, my in-laws George and Heather, my lovely nieces and nephews and cousins (especially James for your superb insights into Gen Z) and of course Auntie V. And Pops, because I know you would have loved all this nonsense.

Huge gratitude to my girlfriends, the ones who are mentioned in this book, but also the many other ones who have been so encouraging – even a 'How's the book going?' message on WhatsApp meant a lot. I'm lucky to have so many brilliant women around me, we lift each other up, as we should. And speaking of friends, a mention for Scott, because he always, always has my back.

Emily MacDonald, my agent – I am so grateful for your guidance, patience and inspiration (we did it!). Thank you also to Julia Eagleton and Katie Bond for seeing the potential in the idea, and to the Aurum team, especially Phoebe, Richard, Liz and Viviane, for bringing it to life so wonderfully.

Special thanks to the excellent people that lent (appropriately) their voices to this story (in order of appearance): Professor Clive Bonsall, Tessa Clarke, Alexandra Walsh, Annie Gray, Mark Peterson, Chris Blazina, Josh Nickell, Shannon Cutts, Alan Pisarski, Susan Shaheen, Rob Brown, Nathan Coley, Melanie Backe-Hansen, Anne Dvinge, Laura Arciniegas, Dr Amy Miller and Lieke van Kerkhoven. And an extra thank you to Dr Matt Cole of Birmingham University History Department for taking such an interest in the book and being so generous with his time and ideas. I'd also like to mention Chloe Duckworth, Ozan Atsiz, Richard Dilks, Brendan Doody, John Hannavy and anyone else who kindly spared their time but whose words didn't make the final edit.

Thank you also to Neal Gorenflo, Steve and Darren Cody, Daan Weddephol, Mike Rosenbaum, Josh Kline, Zelani Bhuiyan, Marianne Olsson, Harmen van Sprang, Lars Ronning, Rebecca Heaps and Kapila Perera (and others mentioned elsewhere) for helping with my sharing guides.

I also really want to thank Jeremy Gottschalk for being such a cheerleader for everything I do, as well as a true friend; Andrea Antoniou (my spirit animal) and all of the Marketplace Risk team, Advisory Board and community; Juliet Eccleston (one of the first people to read this) and the Sharing Economy UK council and members, especially Emma McConalogue, Elizabeth Benaya for her support and friendship throughout this project, Claes Persson, whose 'anything is possible' energy will stay with me even though he is no longer around; Mark Peterson and team Ziscuit, Gina Farish, Mel Morris and last, but certainly not least, my best friend Fiona Neilson.